As of January 12, 2012, this guidance applies to federal savings associations in addition to national banks.*

O-Der

Comptroller of the Currency
Administrator of National Banks

I0448313

Risk Management of Financial Derivatives

Comptroller's Handbook

Narrative - January 1997, Procedures - February 1998

Other Areas of Examination Interest

As of January 12, 2012, this guidance applies to federal savings associations in addition to national banks.*

Risk Management of Financial Derivatives

Table of Contents

Risk Management
of Financial Derivatives

Introduction

Background

Market deregulation, growth in global trade, and continuing technological developments have revolutionized the financial marketplace during the past two decades. A by-product of this revolution is increased market volatility, which has led to a corresponding increase in demand for risk management products. This demand is reflected in the growth of financial derivatives from the standardized futures and options products of the 1970s to the wide spectrum of over-the-counter (OTC) products offered and sold in the 1990s.

Many products and instruments are often described as derivatives by the financial press and market participants. In this guidance, financial derivatives are broadly defined as instruments that primarily derive their value from the performance of underlying interest or foreign exchange rates, equity, or commodity prices.

Financial derivatives come in many shapes and forms, including futures, forwards, swaps, options, structured debt obligations and deposits, and various combinations thereof. Some are traded on organized exchanges, whereas others are privately negotiated transactions. Derivatives have become an integral part of the financial markets because they can serve several economic functions. Derivatives can be used to reduce business risks, expand product offerings to customers, trade for profit, manage capital and funding costs, and alter the risk-reward profile of a particular item or an entire balance sheet.

Although derivatives are legitimate and valuable tools for banks, like all financial instruments they contain risks that must be managed. Managing these risks should not be considered unique or singular. Rather, doing so should be integrated into the bank's overall risk management structure. Risks associated with derivatives are not new or exotic. They are basically the same as those faced in traditional activities (e.g., price, interest rate, liquidity, credit risk). Fundamentally, the risk of derivatives (as of all financial instruments) is a function of the timing and variability of cash flows.

There have been several widely publicized reports on large derivative losses experienced by banks and corporations. Contributing to these losses were inadequate board and senior management oversight, excessive risk-taking, insufficient understanding of the products, and poor internal controls. These events serve as a reminder of the importance of understanding the various risk factors associated with business activities and establishing appropriate risk management systems to identify, measure, monitor, and control exposure.

Risks Associated with Derivative Activities

Risk is the potential that events, expected or unanticipated, may have an adverse impact on the bank's capital and earnings. The OCC has defined nine categories of risk for bank supervision purposes. These risks are: strategic, reputation, price, foreign exchange, liquidity, interest rate, credit, transaction, and compliance. These categories are not mutually exclusive. Any product or service may expose the bank to multiple risks. For analysis and discussion purposes, however, the OCC identifies and assesses each risk separately. Derivative activities must be managed with consideration of all of these risks.

Use of This Guidance

This guidance is intended to provide a framework for evaluating the adequacy of risk management practices of derivative dealers and end-users. Although this guidance is comprehensive in scope, it provides only a framework. Bankers and examiners must still exercise judgment when determining whether risk management processes are appropriate. Also, while this guidance specifically addresses derivatives, many of the risk management concepts described herein can (and should) be applied to other risk-taking activities.

The main body of this guidance provides an overview of sound risk management practices for derivatives. More technical information on the various aspects of derivatives risk management, such as evaluating statistical models, is available in the appendix.

Separate examination procedures, internal control questions, and verification procedures are provided for dealers and end-users. The examination procedures are designed to be comprehensive. At many banks, some of these procedures will not apply. Examiners should tailor the procedures to a bank's activities.

This guidance reflects the policies communicated in the following documents issued by the OCC:

- Banking Circular 277: "Risk Management of Financial Derivatives"
- OCC Bulletin 94-32: "Questions and Answers About BC-277"
- OCC Advisory Letter 94-2: "Purchases of Structured Notes"
- Comptroller's Handbook: "Futures Commission Merchant Activities"
- Comptroller's Handbook: "Emerging Market Country Products and Trading Activities"
- OCC Bulletin 96-25: "Fiduciary Risk Management of Derivatives and Mortgage-Backed Securities"
- OCC Bulletin 96-36: "Interest Rate Risk"
- OCC Bulletin 96-43: "Credit Derivatives"

These guidelines and procedures focus principally on *off-balance-sheet* derivatives and structured notes. OCC policy on evaluating the risks in more traditional cash products with derivative characteristics (e.g., mortgage-related holdings and loans with caps/floors, etc.) is available in other sections of the *Comptroller's Handbook*. Examiners and bankers evaluating derivative activities at national banks should also consult, as applicable, the following sections of the *Comptroller's Handbook*: "Interest Rate Risk Management," "Investment Portfolio Management," "Emerging Market Country Products and Trading Activities," "Futures Commission Merchant Activities," and "Fiduciary and Asset Management Activities."

Roles Banks Take in Derivative Activities

National banks participating in the derivative markets function in two general roles: dealer and end-user. These two roles are not mutually exclusive; in most cases, a bank that functions as a derivative dealer will also be an end-user.

Dealers

A bank that markets derivative products to customers is considered a dealer. For purposes of this guidance, the OCC has classified dealers into two types.

Tier I. A Tier I dealer acts as a market-maker, providing quotes to other dealers and brokers, and other market professionals. Tier I dealers may also take proprietary positions in derivatives in anticipation of changes in prices or volatility. Tier I dealers actively solicit customer business, often using a dedicated sales force. These dealers also develop new derivative products. Typically, they have systems and personnel that allow them to tailor derivatives to the needs of their customers. Large portfolios, complex contracts, and high transaction volume distinguish Tier I dealers from other market participants.

Tier II. The primary difference between Tier I and Tier II dealers is that Tier II dealers are not market-makers. Tier II dealers tend to restrict quotes to a select customer base even though they may have a high volume of transactions. Tier II dealers typically do not actively develop new products. Tier II dealers may match or offset their customer transactions with other dealers or professional counterparties or they may choose to manage risk on an aggregate basis.

Throughout this guidance, the terms dealer and dealing will collectively refer to both customer and proprietary trading activities.

End-Users

An end-user engages in derivative transactions for its own account. An end-user may use derivatives as a substitute for cash market investments, a tool for interest rate risk management, or for other balance sheet management purposes. In this guidance, the OCC has classified end-users into two types, which are defined below.

Active Position-Taker. This type of end-user employs derivatives to dynamically manage risk, either to reduce risk or purposefully increase the risk profile of the institution. Active position-takers often use derivatives as surrogates for cash market instruments. These banks generally have large derivative positions relative to their total asset size. They also tend to use more complex derivative structures than other end-users.

Limited End-User. Limited end-users are characterized by smaller portfolios and lower transaction volume than active position-takers. This type of end-user primarily uses derivatives as an investment alternative or to manage interest rate risk. Many limited end-users engage in derivatives solely through ownership of structured notes in their investment portfolios. These banks tend to use simpler, more mature products (although certain structured notes may be extremely complex and illiquid).

The following chart may be useful in distinguishing among participants in derivative markets:

Derivative Activity	Tier I Dealer	Tier II Dealer	Active Position-Taker	Limited End-User
Provides quotes to dealers	X			
Develops new products	X			
Provides quotes to customers	X	X		
Uses complex structures	X	X	X	*
Frequently engages in derivative transactions	X	X	X	
Acts as principal	X	X	X	X
Takes position risk	X	X	X	X
Uses mature products	X	X	X	X

*Although limited end-users generally tend to use simpler products, some have purchased certain structured notes that may be extremely complex and illiquid.

Senior Management and Board Oversight

The safe and sound use of derivatives is contingent upon effective senior management and board oversight. It is the responsibility of the board to hire a competent executive management team, endorse the corporate vision and the overall business strategy (including the institutional risk appetite), and hold executive management accountable for performance. The board must understand the role derivatives play in the overall business strategy.

It is the responsibility of senior management to ensure the development of risk management systems. This entails developing and implementing a sound risk management framework composed of policies and procedures, risk measurement and reporting systems, and independent oversight and control processes.

The formality of senior management and board oversight mechanisms will differ depending on the derivatives activities conducted by the bank. However, the board and senior management must provide adequate resources (financial, technical expertise, and systems technology) to implement appropriate oversight mechanisms.

The management of derivative activities should be integrated into the bank's overall risk management system using a conceptual framework common to the bank's other businesses. For example, the price risk exposure from derivative transactions should be assessed in a comparable manner to and aggregated with all other price risk exposures. Risk consolidation is particularly important because the various risks contained in derivatives and other market activities can be interconnected and may transcend specific markets.

Policies and Procedures

A bank's policies should provide a framework for the management of risk. Dealers and active position-takers should have written policies for derivative activities to ensure proper identification, quantification, evaluation, and control of risks. Banks whose derivative activities are limited in volume, scope, and nature may not need the formality of written policies and procedures provided that the board and senior management have established and communicated clear goals, objectives, authorities, and controls for this activity.

Derivative policies need not be stand-alone documents. Rather, derivative-related guidelines can be included in policies that control financial risk-taking (e.g., price, interest rate, liquidity, and credit risk) on an aggregate bank level, as well as at the functional business unit or product level. Operating, accounting, compliance, and capital management policies should also address the use of derivatives.

Senior management should ensure that policies identify managerial oversight, assign clear responsibility, and require development and implementation of procedures to guide the bank's daily activities. Policies should detail authorized activities, as well as activities that require one-off approval and activities that are considered inappropriate. Policies should articulate the risk tolerance of the bank in terms of comprehensive risk limits, and require regular risk position and performance reporting.

When developing policies and controls for derivative activities, senior management should not overlook the bank's use of derivatives in a fiduciary capacity. Fiduciary policies are usually separate from the commercial bank policies because of business and customer privacy considerations. National banks that purchase derivative instruments for fiduciary accounts should fully understand the associated credit, interest rate, liquidity, price, and transaction risks of such instruments. Additionally, national bank fiduciaries should consider the compliance and reputation risks presented by investing fiduciary assets in derivatives, and the appropriateness of derivative instruments for customer accounts.

Policies must keep pace with the changing nature of derivative products and markets. On an ongoing basis, the board or appropriate committee should review and endorse significant changes in derivative activities. At least annually, the board, or a designated committee, should also approve key policy statements. Meeting minutes should document these actions. (Note: Given the extent and nature of demands placed on the board, committees may be created to handle matters requiring detailed review or in-depth consideration, with each committee reporting to the board. Accordingly, the words board and committee are used synonymously throughout this document.)

New Products

Before transacting new types of derivative products, senior management should comprehensively analyze the new product or activity. A mechanism to capture and report all new products is critical to the board and senior management's ability to execute proper oversight of the bank's risk profile.

New products frequently require different pricing, processing, accounting, and risk measurement systems. Management and the board must ensure that adequate knowledge, staffing, technology, and financial resources exist to accommodate the activity. Furthermore, plans to enter new markets/products should consider the cost of establishing appropriate controls, as well as attracting professional staff with the necessary expertise.

The new product approval process should include a sign-off by all relevant areas such as risk control, operations, accounting, legal, audit, and senior and line management. Depending on the magnitude of the new product or activity and its impact on the bank's risk profile, senior management, and in some cases, the board, should provide the final approval.

For new as well as existing products, a uniform product assessment process should be part of the overall risk management function. The goal of this process should be to ensure that all significant risks and issues are addressed. Elements that should be included in a uniform product assessment are listed in appendix A.

Defining a product or activity as new is central to ensuring that variations on existing products receive the proper review and authorization. Factors that should be considered when deciding whether or not a product must be routed through the new-product process include, but are not limited to: capacity changes (e.g., end-user to dealer), structure variations (e.g., non-amortizing swap versus amortizing interest rate swap), products which require a new pricing methodology, legal or regulatory considerations (e.g., the requirement to obtain OCC approval of the bank's plan to engage in physical commodity transactions), and market characteristics (e.g., foreign exchange forwards in major currencies as opposed to emerging market currencies).

When in doubt as to whether a product requires compliance with the new-product approval process, bank management should err on the side of conservatism and apply the process to the proposed product or activity.

Oversight Mechanisms

A bank's board of directors and senior management can readily approve policies delineating permissible derivative activities and risk tolerances. However, the volume and complexity of activities at many banks makes it impractical for these directors and senior management to oversee the day-to-day management of derivative activities. Consequently, they rely on strong risk control and audit functions to ensure compliance with policies.

The risk control and audit functions should possess the independence, authority, and corporate stature to be unimpeded in identifying and reporting their findings. It is equally important to employ individuals with sufficient experience and technical expertise to be credible to the business line they monitor and senior executives to whom they report. Evaluations of these employees and their compensation should be independent of the businesses they monitor and audit.

Risk Control

The role and structure of the risk control function (also referred to as market risk management at banks with significant trading activities) should be commensurate with the extent and complexity of the derivative activities. Because measuring and controlling the risk of some derivative activities can be more complex than doing so for traditional products, a strong risk control function is a key element in assisting board members and senior managers in fulfilling their oversight responsibilities.

Risk control units should regularly evaluate risk-taking activities by assessing risk levels and the adequacy of risk management processes. These units should also monitor the development and implementation of control policies and risk measurement systems. Risk control personnel staff should periodically communicate their observations to senior management and the board.

Depending on the nature and extent of a bank's activities, the risk control function can be structured in various ways. At banks with significant derivative activities, the risk control function should be a separate unit reporting directly to the board or a board committee. If independence is not compromised, this unit may report to a senior executive with no direct responsibility for derivative activities.

Banks with smaller and less complex derivative activities may not find it economically feasible to establish a separate risk control unit. Often the most practical solution for such banks is the use of independent treasury support units, or qualified outside auditors or consultants. These individuals report risk-taking and management issues to the board or a committee, such as an Asset Liability Management Committee (ALCO). The selected approach should be structured to ensure sufficient stature and expertise in the oversight role.

Audit

Audits should be conducted by qualified professionals who are independent of the business line being audited. Audits should supplement, and not be a substitute for, a risk control function.

The scope of audit coverage should be commensurate with the level of risk and volume of activity. The audit should include an appraisal of the adequacy of operations, compliance, and accounting systems and the effectiveness of internal controls. Auditors should test compliance with the bank's policies, including limits. The audit should include an evaluation of the reliability and timeliness of information reported to senior management and the board of directors. Auditors should trace and verify information provided on risk exposure reports to the underlying data sources. The audit should include an appraisal of the effectiveness and independence of the risk management process. Auditors might ensure that risk measurement models, including algorithms, are properly validated. The audit should include an evaluation of the adequacy of the derivative valuation process and ensure that it is performed by parties independent of risk-taking activities. Auditors should test derivative valuation reports for accuracy. For hedge transactions, auditors should review the appropriateness of accounting treatment and test for compliance with accounting policies.

Procedures should be in place to ensure that auditors are informed of significant changes in product lines, risk management methods, risk limits, operating systems, and internal controls so that they can update their procedures and revise their audit scope accordingly. Auditors should periodically review and analyze performance and risk management reports to ensure that areas showing significant changes (e.g., earnings or risk levels) are given appropriate attention.

The level of auditor expertise should also be consistent with the level and complexity of activities and degree of risk assumed. In many cases, banks choose to out-source audit coverage to ensure that the professionals performing the work possess sufficient knowledge and experience.

The audit function must have the support of management and the board in order to be effective. Management should respond promptly to audit findings by investigating identified system and internal control weaknesses and implementing corrective action. Thereafter, management should periodically monitor newly implemented systems and controls to ensure they are working appropriately. The board, or designated committee, should receive reports tracking management's actions to address identified deficiencies.

Risk Measurement

Accurate measurement of derivative-related risks is necessary for proper monitoring and control. All significant risks should be measured and integrated into a bank-wide or corporate-wide risk management system. For example, price risk measurement should incorporate exposure from derivatives, as well as cash products.

Measurement of some types of risk is an approximation. Certain risks, such as liquidity risk, can be very difficult to quantify precisely and can vary with economic and market conditions. At a minimum, management should regularly assess vulnerabilities to these risks in response to changing circumstances. The sophistication and precision of risk measurement methods will vary by the types, volumes, and riskiness of the activities. Various types of risk measurement methods are discussed later in this guidance within each risk section (e.g., sections on price, credit, and liquidity risk).

Risk Limits

Risk limits serve as a means to control exposures to the various risks associated with derivative activities. Limits should be integrated across the bank and measured against aggregate (e.g., individual and geographical) risks. Limits should be compatible with the nature of the bank's strategies, risk measurement systems, and the board's risk tolerance. To ensure consistency between limits and business strategies, the board should annually approve limits as part of the overall budget process. Outside the annual approval process, changes in resources or market conditions should prompt the board to reassess limits and make appropriate revisions. Annual approvals of limits and any interim revisions should be communicated to appropriate parties within the bank (e.g., traders, risk managers, operations, and audit).

In addition to providing a means of controlling aggregate exposure, limits can be used to foster communication of position strategies and changes in the bank's risk profile. Limits called management action triggers are often used for this purpose.

Line managers should not wait until a limit is broken to alert senior management and risk control units. Instead, they should promptly report unanticipated changes and progressively deteriorating positions, as well as other significant issues arising from their positions, to the risk control function and responsible management.

When reviewing a bank's limit structure, examiners should evaluate the size of limits in relation to the bank's capital base, earnings, and the board's expressed risk tolerance. The risks resulting from full utilization of a bank's limits should not compromise the financial condition of the bank. In addition, the size of the limits should be consistent with the board's philosophy towards risk. Examiners should also analyze the percentage of limit utilization over time. Excessively large limits in relation to normal risk levels and limit usage can fail to convey meaningful shifts in risk-taking activity and can fail to trigger a formal evaluation process. Conversely, overly restrictive limits that are frequently exceeded may undermine the purpose of the limit structure.

Risk-Adjusted Return Analysis

As measurement and performance systems have continued to develop, techniques to evaluate business risks and corresponding earnings performance have evolved. The ability to measure and assess the risk-return relationship of various businesses has resulted in further steps to measure the risk-adjusted return on capital. This analysis allows senior management to judge whether the financial performance of individual business units justifies the risks undertaken.

The capacity to allocate risk-adjusted capital to the business units requires systems to comprehensively measure the inherent risks associated with the risk-taking activity. Internal financial reporting systems should be able to attribute risks and earnings to their appropriate sources. Management should measure earnings against capital allocated to the activity, adjusted for price, interest rate, credit, liquidity, transaction, and other risks.

The industry is in various stages of implementing and refining methods of calculating risk-adjusted return. The development of internal risk measurement systems, calculation of risk-based capital charges, and the internal allocation of revenue and expenses are some of the requirements necessary for implementing such a process. As risk-adjusted evaluation techniques evolve, management will increasingly rely on this tool for business evaluation. However, this should be one tool of several used to assess the performance of a unit; others are management judgment and an understanding of the profit dynamics and the implied value-added aspects of the business activity.

Affiliates

Many multibank holding companies elect to manage risks by conducting derivative transactions with their affiliates rather than external counterparties. Such strategies centralize control of price and credit exposures, reduce transaction costs, and decrease the risks (e.g., credit and compliance) of dealing with external counterparties.

The board and senior management should ensure that policies and procedures are established to address derivative transactions with affiliates. The policy should describe the nature of acceptable affiliate transactions, pricing, monitoring, and reporting. Senior management should ensure that affiliate transactions comply with this policy.

Management Information Systems

The frequency and composition of board and management reporting should depend upon the nature and significance of derivative activities. Where applicable, board and management reports should consolidate information across functional and geographic divisions.

Board and management reporting should be tailored to the intended audience, providing summary information to senior management and the board and more detailed information to line management. For example, the board, or designated committee, should periodically receive information illustrating trends in aggregate exposure, compliance with business strategies and risk limits, and risk-adjusted return performance. Line management should receive more detailed reports with sufficient information to assess risk levels, returns, and the consistency with strategic objectives. Examples of types of reports that the board and management should receive are listed in each of the major sections of this guidance.

Ideally, management reports should be generated by control departments independent of the risk-takers. When risk-takers provide information (e.g., valuations or volatilities on thinly traded derivative contracts) for management reports, senior management should be informed of possible weaknesses in the data, and these positions should be audited frequently.

Personnel and Compensation Plans

Because of their increased complexity, derivative activities require a highly skilled staff particularly in the risk-taking, risk control, and operational functions. Management should regularly review the knowledge, skills, and number of people needed to engage in existing and new derivative activities. They should also ensure that the staff is appropriately balanced and that no area is understaffed in terms of skill or number.

Staff turnover can create serious problems, especially if knowledge is concentrated in a few individuals. Periodic rotation and cross-training of staff members performing key functions can help build depth over time and alleviate some of this risk. In addition, contingency plans should be established addressing the loss of key personnel. Contingency actions may include curtailing existing or new activities or outsourcing functions to qualified auditors or consultants.

The impact of staff turnover can be particularly acute in specialized trading markets where traders are in high demand and are often recruited in teams. Movement of entire teams can lead to a lack of business continuity and heightened exposure to intellectual risk. To encourage trader retention, some banks have implemented deferred payment/bonus programs, often referred to as golden handcuffs.

Personnel policies should require employees who are in positions that can significantly affect the books and records of the bank to take two consecutive weeks of leave each year. The importance of implementing this control has been confirmed by recent well publicized trading losses that occurred because traders were able to conceal unauthorized trading activities for a number of years without being detected. These unauthorized activities might have been detected earlier if the traders had been required to take leave. Employees subject to this policy should not be able to effect any transactions while on leave. Exceptions to this policy should be granted only after careful consideration and approval by senior management. In no instance should multiple exceptions for the same employee be allowed to occur.

Management should ensure that compensation programs are sufficient to recruit and retain experienced staff. However, compensation programs should not encourage excessive risk-taking. Because of the leverage and volatility associated with derivatives and the consequent ability to generate large profits in a relatively short time, employees may be tempted to take excessive risk. Therefore, it is important that compensation programs do not motivate an employee to take risk that is incompatible with corporate strategies, risk appetite, policies, or applicable laws and regulations. Compensation that is based on short-term results may not take into account long-term risks.

When establishing compensation programs and determining specific payments (such as bonuses), senior management should consider:

- Individual overall performance.

- Performance relative to the bank's stated goals.

- Risk-adjusted return.

- Compliance with bank policies, laws, and regulations.

- Competitors' compensation packages for similar responsibilities and performance.

Strategic Risk

Strategic risk is the risk to earnings or capital arising from adverse business decisions or improper implementation of those decisions. This risk is a function of the compatibility between an organization's strategic goals, the business strategies developed to achieve those goals, the resources deployed in pursuit of these goals, and the quality of implementation. The resources needed to carry out business strategies are both tangible and intangible. They include communication channels, operating systems, delivery networks, and managerial capacities and capabilities.

Strategic risk may arise when the bank's business approach is not well developed or properly executed because of: an inability to react to changes in market condition, shifts in internal management focus, lack of internal coordination and communication to facilitate product delivery, or an inability to assemble the necessary financial, personnel, and systems infrastructure. Proper strategic planning and consistent market approach are integral to the success of the product or business activity.

The management of strategic risk involves more than development of the strategic plan. It also focuses on how plans, systems, and implementation affect the value of the institution. It includes analyses of external factors affecting the bank's strategic direction and analyses of the success of past business strategies.

A bank's derivative activities should be part of the bank's overall business strategy, which has been endorsed by the board. This strategy may be articulated within policies governing other activities or documented separately. Strategy statements should include the following:

- Scope of activities.

- Consistency with bank's overall business strategy.

- Market assessment:

  - Supply/demand.
  - Competitive factors.

- − Niche or role and anticipated level of activity.
- − Target market/customers.

- Projected risk/reward payoff.

- Business evaluation and performance benchmarks.

- Personnel and systems needs.

Business strategies should be communicated to appropriate levels within the bank to ensure consistent understanding and implementation.

Reputation Risk

Reputation risk is the risk to earnings or capital arising from negative public opinion. This affects the institution's ability to establish new relationships or services, or continue servicing existing relationships. This risk can expose the institution to litigation, financial loss, or damage to its reputation. Reputation risk is present throughout the organization and includes the responsibility to exercise an abundance of caution in dealing with its customers and community. This risk is present in such activities as asset management and agency transactions.

Because the orderly operation of financial markets is largely based on confidence among all market participants, banks that actively associate their name with financial products such as derivatives are more likely to have higher reputation risk. Derivative activities carry a higher degree of reputation risk because they are generally more complex and less understood by the public than other financial products. If the bank engages in a derivative transaction that is inappropriate for the customer or that the customer does not understand, there is greater potential for customer default, litigation, and damage to the bank's reputation.

Banks acting in an agency capacity may not have the same legal obligations as a principal, but are subject to reputation risk. To diminish this risk, sound risk management principles require the bank to determine whether transactions are appropriate for agency customers. Banks that act as a fiduciary are also subject to reputation risk. When engaging in derivative transactions in a fiduciary capacity, the bank has a duty to ensure that the contracts are appropriate for the beneficiaries and consistent with prudent man investment standards. See the "Credit Risk" section for more information on customer appropriateness.

Management of reputation risk begins with fostering a know-your-customer culture within the institution. Senior management should adopt a code of conduct that addresses such areas as conflicts of interest, customer confidentiality, sales practices, appropriateness, illegal and improper payments, and insider trading. Management should encourage compliance with policies through employee affirmations, standardized disclosures, and appropriate testing processes. The administration of prompt and consistent disciplinary action against infractions will also help to foster a strong compliance culture. Senior management should continually assess the compatibility of bank activities and employee compensation programs with the code of conduct.

Price Risk (Tier I and Tier II Dealers)

Price risk is the risk to earnings or capital arising from changes in the value of portfolios of financial instruments. This risk arises from market-making, dealing, and position-taking activities for interest rate, foreign exchange, equity and commodity markets. Many banks use the term price risk interchangeably with market risk. The primary accounts affected by price risk are those that are revalued for financial presentation (e.g., trading accounts for securities, derivatives, and foreign exchange products).

Dealers are exposed to price risk to the degree they have unhedged exposure relating to customer trades or proprietary positions. The degree of price risk depends on the price sensitivity of the derivative instrument and the time it takes to liquidate or offset (close out) the position. Price sensitivity is generally greater for instruments with leverage, longer maturities, or option features. In deep, liquid markets the time it takes to close out a position is usually assumed to be at most one business day. In less liquid markets, it may take much longer.

Types of Price Risk

The primary factors that affect the price of derivative contracts are interest rates, foreign exchange rates, equity prices, and commodity prices. In addition to the absolute changes in these factors, the volatility of those changes can influence the prices of derivative products that have option or leverage features.

When evaluating the sensitivity of a derivative contract to a change in price risk factors, the contract's terms, maturity, and timing and amount of future cashflows must be considered. When evaluating the potential impact on a portfolio of contracts, the extent to which contracts may complement or offset one another should also be considered.

Price risk factors and pertinent aspects of options and leveraged products are discussed below.

Interest Rates

The magnitude of the exposure from an adverse change in interest rates depends on the sensitivity of the instrument to changes in interest rates as well as the absolute change in interest rates. In general, values of long-term instruments are more sensitive to interest rate changes than the values of short-term instruments.

Interest rate exposure can arise from either a parallel shift in the yield curve (term structure exposure) or a change in the shape of the yield curve (yield curve twist exposure).

Foreign Exchange Rates

The exposure from an adverse change in foreign exchange rates is a function of spot foreign exchange rates and domestic and foreign interest rates. Any forward premium or discount in the value of a foreign currency relative to the domestic currency is determined largely by relative interest rates. Foreign exchange rates can be and have been very volatile (e.g., EMS crisis of 1992).

Equity Prices

The exposure from an adverse change in equity prices is usually classified as either systematic or unsystematic (security-specific) risk. Systematic risk arises from an event (of any magnitude) that affects all equities simultaneously. For example, when the economy is growing, all equities will likely be affected either in a cyclical (e.g., luxury goods) or countercyclical (e.g., discount stores) fashion. Unsystematic risk represents price risk unique to the equity of a particular company (and its equity derivatives). Equity markets can be more volatile than other financial markets; therefore, equity derivatives can experience larger price fluctuations than other financial derivatives.

When assessing price risk arising from equity derivatives, the distinction between systematic and unsystematic risk is an important consideration. Unsystematic risk can be reduced by diversification. Because the returns of different instruments can be negatively correlated, the total volatility of a portfolio of instruments may be less than the summed volatility of the component instruments. Moreover, in a well-diversified portfolio, any one asset represents a small fraction of the total portfolio and, consequently, an insignificant portion of total portfolio variance. Systematic risk cannot be reduced by diversification, because a market move will affect all security prices in a similar way (albeit to varying degrees).

Commodity Prices

Like equity derivatives, commodity derivatives usually expose an institution to higher levels of price risk than other financial derivatives, because of the price volatility associated with uncertainties about supply and demand and the concentration of market participants in the underlying cash markets. Because of these market characteristics, the commodity derivative markets are generally much less liquid than the interest rate and foreign exchange markets (where there are a large number of market participants), and fluctuations in market liquidity often accompany price volatility. An evaluation of exposure to adverse changes in commodity prices should be performed on a market-by-market basis. Depending on the level and nature of commodity exposure, this evaluation may include an analysis of historical price behavior and an assessment of the structure of market supply and demand to evaluate the potential for unusually large price movements.

Basis Risk

Basis risk is the risk that the correlation between two prices may change. (Correlation is the relationship between mathematical or statistical variables.) For example, if a bank uses an interest rate swap priced off of Libor to hedge a prime-based loan portfolio, it is exposed to basis risk because changes in prime and Libor will not move exactly in tandem with each other.

Similarly, changes in the values of certain foreign currencies can be correlated under normal market conditions but these correlations can be unstable during volatile market periods. For example, if a bank uses a derivative denominated in one foreign currency to hedge an asset denominated in another foreign currency, it exposes itself to basis risk even when those currencies have been historically closely correlated.

Option Characteristics

The value of an option is the function of several variables, including the current spot price of the underlying asset, the volatility of the price of the underlying asset, interest rates, time to expiration, and the option's exercise price.

The potential exposure from options is measured by evaluating the sensitivity of options prices to changes in price risk factors. Sensitivity or exposure can be measured in aggregate (i.e., the total value of the option) or in components. These components are referred to as "the Greeks," because most of them are designated by letters of the Greek alphabet.

The primary component measures of options sensitivity are:

Delta – the sensitivity of an option's value to changes in the price of the underlying instrument.

Gamma – the amount delta would change in response to a change in the price of the underlying instrument.

Vega (also known as **kappa**) – the sensitivity of an option's price to changes in the volatility of the underlying instrument.

Theta – the amount an option's price would be expected to change to reflect the passage of time (also called time decay).

Rho – the amount an option's price would change for an incremental move (generally one basis point) in short-term interest rates.

Much more information on "the Greeks" and how they are used for risk management purposes can be found in appendix B.

Because options give the purchaser the right, but not the obligation, to engage in a specified transaction, the payoff from options is asymmetric. Purchasers would only exercise an option to experience a gain. Should markets move adversely, holders of options would not experience a loss over time (other than the loss of the premium paid). Such a risk-reward profile, potentially unlimited upside gain with limited downside cost (the premium paid), creates an asymmetric payoff for options. The reverse would hold true of sellers (writers) of options contracts, who would benefit from limited revenue (the premium received for the option) and be exposed to potentially unlimited downside loss.

Effect of Leverage

The price sensitivity of a derivative contract is magnified by the effects of leverage. By definition, derivative contracts are leveraged because for a relatively small performance bond (e.g., margin) or premium, a counterparty can enter into a transaction that possesses the risk/return tradeoff of a much larger dollar volume of the underlying cash instrument. Small changes in the underlying price factor can produce a large change in the value of the derivative. Leverage can be intensified when the cash flow of a contract is based on some multiple of the performance of the underlying cash instrument. The price sensitivity of contracts containing leverage factors can be extremely high.

Price Risk Management

Dealers involved in derivative activities must establish an effective process for managing price risk. The level of structure and formality associated with this process should be commensurate with the level of risk in the bank's activities.
Key components of price risk management systems include:

- Reliable and independent pricing and revaluation systems.

- Accurate and validated risk measurement processes.
- Stress testing to show how the portfolio would perform under certain extreme events.

- Meaningful processes for establishing price risk limits.

- Timely and effective risk reporting, monitoring, and exception approval processes.

Pricing and Revaluation Systems

Derivative dealers need pricing and revaluation systems to effectively manage exposure to price risk factors. These systems (and price risk measurement systems discussed below) require similar input data that describe the derivative contract's terms, maturity, and expected cash flow. These systems may be the same, integrated, or separate.

Pricing system(s) are used to determine reliable prices for derivative products being purchased and sold. Such pricing systems allow dealers to evaluate prices offered in the market, identify profits and losses on positions, and identify potential risks in the portfolio. A pricing system is often developed by the business using the system. In these situations, the systems should be maintained by an independent party and subject to a rigorous validation process. Validation is discussed later and in appendix D.

Revaluation systems provide mark-to-market information for reporting positions and recording profits and losses. It is imperative that the input used for determining the fair value of positions and profits/losses be independent of risk-taking personnel (see the "Transaction Risk" section for further comments on periodic revaluations).

Banks should regularly review their pricing and revaluation models to ensure they provide a reasonable estimate of value. In addition, banks should continually monitor acceptance of the pricing model's results in the marketplace. If the model's results are inconsistent with the market, banks must decide whether to continue using the model.

Price Risk Measurement

There are a variety of ways to measure price risk, some of which are far more sophisticated than others. The degree of sophistication in price risk measurement should be related to (1) the type and amount of price risk, (2) the ability of management to understand the nature, limitations, and meaning of the measurement and (3) the nature of trading activities. The less sophisticated methods are only appropriate when a bank uses conservative strategies, the level of price risk is low relative to earnings and capital, or price risk is linear (no option exposure). For instance, Tier II dealers with largely matched positions would not be expected to have sophisticated risk measurement systems. Institutions with large or complex derivative activities or large open positions need the more sophisticated measurement methods that rely on mathematical models to replicate price behavior.

Value-at-risk (VAR) is one of the most common methods used by dealer banks to measure aggregate price risk. VAR is an estimate of the potential loss within a specified confidence interval in a portfolio's value over a defined holding period. In trading portfolios that are marked-to-market daily, VAR is usually translated into a potential reduction in the bank's future earnings. VAR is most valuable as a high-level management information tool because it reduces a bank's multiple price risks to a single number or to a small number of key statistics. The trading desks will manage their individual exposures using more detailed information. See the "Evaluating Price Risk Measurement" section for more information on VAR.

Although generally believed to reflect risk more precisely, the more sophisticated price risk measurement systems (as well as pricing and revaluation systems) can introduce the added risk that: (1) the algorithms and assumptions underlying the models are not valid; (2) the models are inappropriately applied; (3) the models are not well understood within the organization; and (4) the model's results are inconsistent with the market (applicable to pricing systems). This is sometimes termed model risk. Banks should regularly re-evaluate risk measurement models and assumptions to ensure they provide reasonable estimates of risks. Management should ensure that the models are used for their intended purpose and not as a proxy because the bank lacks a more appropriate model (see appendix C for more information on evaluating statistical models).

There are six fundamental issues that must be addressed when formulating risk measurement systems. These are: (1) purpose of the measure; (2) position description; (3) holding period; (4) confidence interval (probability threshold); (5) historical time period of the data series; (6) aggregation. These issues are discussed in appendix G.

Evaluating Price Risk Measurement

Banks should regularly re-evaluate risk measurement models to ensure that they provide a reasonable estimate of risk. Management should ensure that the models are used for their intended purpose and that *material limitations of the models* are well understood at appropriate levels within the organization.

Although VAR is the most common method of measuring price risk, it is important that management and the board understand the system's limitations. VAR is appealing to users because it reduces multiple price risks into a single value-at-risk number or a small number of key statistics. However, VAR results are highly dependent upon assumptions, algorithms, and methods. VAR does not provide assurance that the potential loss will fall within a certain confidence interval (e.g., 99 percent); rather, it estimates the potential loss based on a specific set of assumptions.

Another limitation of VAR is that it may not accurately estimate the impact of large market moves. To address these limitations, dealers need to supplement their VAR scenarios with stress testing. Stress testing helps mitigate weaknesses in VAR by focusing on worst case scenarios that may be outside the confidence interval. Stress testing is discussed in appendix E.

Dealers with high price risk should supplement stress testing with an analysis of their exposure to interconnection risk. While stress testing typically considers the movement of single market factors (e.g., interest rates), interconnection risk considers the linkages between markets (e.g., interest rates and foreign exchange rates) and between the types of risk (e.g., price, credit, and liquidity risk). More information on interconnection risk can be found in appendix F.

Most banks use a combination of independent validation, calibration, back-testing, stress testing, and reserves to mitigate potential weaknesses in price risk measurement models. These processes are described in appendixes D and E.

Price Risk Limits

The price risk limit structure should be consistent with the board's risk appetite and the capabilities of the risk measurement system. Institutions should use a variety of limits to adequately capture the range of price risks or to address risks that the measurement system does not capture. A single type of limit is generally not sufficient on its own to control price risk. However, many types of limits tend to complement each other. For instance, aggregate VAR limits are a mechanism to control risk on a bank or entity-wide level. Traders will need supplemental limits (e.g., stop-loss limits) to control risk at the desk or portfolio level. Standard limits used to control price risks are described below.

Value-at-Risk Limits. These sensitivity limits are designed to restrict potential loss to an amount equal to a board-approved percentage of projected earnings or capital. All dealers except Tier II dealers with largely matched positions should use VAR limits.

VAR limits are useful for controlling price risk. However, as discussed in "Evaluating Price Risk Measurement," one limitation of VAR is that the results produced are highly dependent upon the algorithms, assumptions, and methodology used by the model. Changes in any of these elements can produce widely different VAR results. In addition, VAR may be less useful for predicting the effect of large market moves. To address these weaknesses, dealers should complement VAR limits with other types of limits such as notional and loss control limits.

Loss Control Limits. Loss control limits require a specific management action if the defined level of loss is approached or breached. If such limits are exceeded, policy should require that a position be closed out or that a higher level of management be contacted for approval of maintaining the exposure. In many cases, the limits are established to foster communication, rather than limit management's ability to maintain a position. For instance, a position that currently exhibits unrealized losses may continue, in management's estimation, to make economic sense over the time horizon it is expected to be held.

Loss control limits complement other limits. However, they are generally not sufficient by themselves, because they are based on unrealized losses to date and do not measure potential loss exposure. When establishing loss control limits, consideration must be given to the starting point (e.g., date transaction is booked) for measuring the loss and period of time (e.g., day, week, month) over which the cumulative loss is measured.

Tenor or Gap Limits. Tenor (maturity) or gap (repricing) limits are designed to reduce price risk by limiting the maturity and/or controlling the volume of transactions that matures or reprices in a given time period. Such limits can be used to reduce the volatility of derivative revenue or expenses by staggering the maturity and/or repricing, thereby smoothing the effect of changes in market factors affecting price.

Tenor limits can also be useful for liquidity risk control. Generally these limits are expressed in terms of volume and/or amount per measurable time period (e.g., day, week, monthly).

Like loss control limits, tenor or gap limits can be used to supplement other limits, but are not sufficient in isolation. They are not anticipatory and do not provide a reasonable proxy for the price risk.

Notional or Volume Limits. Notional or volume limits are most effective for controlling operational capacity and, in some cases, liquidity risk. Specifically, in the case of exchange-traded futures and options, volume limits on open interest may be advisable in less liquid contracts. Limits on concentrations by strike price and expiration date can facilitate portfolio diversification in large books. In the case of OTC options, these limits should be set in the context of the bank's ability to settle a large number of trades if the options are exercised. Notional limits may be very useful for highly illiquid instruments, such as emerging market issues for which the frequency and volatility of price changes render VAR less useful. Because notional amount and volume of contracts do not provide a reasonable proxy for price (or credit) risk, these limits are not acceptable on a stand-alone basis.

Options Limits. Limits specific to option exposure should be established for any dealer with sizable option positions. Such limits should consider the sensitivity of positions to changes in delta, gamma, vega, theta, and rho. Generally, this type of analysis requires the modeling capabilities addressed in the previous discussion of VAR limits.

Product Concentration Limits. Product concentration limits may be useful to ensure that a concentration in any one product does not significantly increase the price risk of the portfolio as a whole.

Management Information Systems

As mentioned earlier, the OCC believes that risk measurement and assessment should be conducted on an aggregate basis. The board and management should evaluate price risks for the bank as a whole, in addition to consideration of other risks.

At least annually, Tier I dealers and Tier II dealers who assume material price risk should present a *summary* of current risk measurement and reporting techniques and management practices to senior management. This presentation should explicitly identify and report not only the advantages of the given models/systems of choice but also the limitations or weaknesses inherent to the given process (for instance, a duration-based model will not incorporate an instrument's convexity or recognize correlations). Also, significant revisions to models should be reported and the impact on risk levels quantified.

The following list includes the types of reports that Tier I and Tier II dealers with material price risk should generate to properly communicate risk. The formality and frequency of reporting should be directly related to the level of derivative activities and risk. The recipients of these reports may also vary depending on the bank organizational structure.

- Board:

    - Trends in aggregate price risk.
    - Compliance with board-approved policies and risk limits.
    - Summary of performance relative to objectives that articulates risk adjusted return.
    - Results of stress testing.
    - Summary of current risk measurement techniques and management practices (annually).

- Asset/Liability Management Committee or other executive management committee responsible for the supervision of price risk:

    - Trends in exposure to applicable price risk factors (e.g., interest rates, volatilities, etc).
    - Compliance with policies and aggregate limits by major business/region.
    - Summary of performance relative to objectives that articulates risk-adjusted return.
    - Major new product developments or business initiatives.
    - Results of stress testing including major assumptions.
    - Summary of current risk measurement techniques and management practices, including results of validation and back-testing exercises (annually).

- Dealers will also need the following reports, as applicable:

Business head/region:

- Detailed profit and loss statement (P&L) by desk.
- Summary of major exposures.
- Compliance with policies and procedures, including limits. Should detail exception frequency and trends.
- Aggregate exposure versus limits.
- Summary of performance relative to objectives that articulates risk-adjusted return.
- Valuation reserve summary.
- Major new product developments or business initiatives.
- Results of stress testing including major assumptions.
- Periodic reports on price risk model development. Should include independent certifications and periodic validation and back-testing of models.

Dealing room:

- Detailed P&L, by desk.
- Sensitivity modeling of significant exposures, e.g., position reports. These can be selected by management or the risk control group, and should include a sensitivity matrix indicating the vulnerability of the position to various changes in the variables affecting price.
- Compliance with limits.
- Summary of performance versus objectives that articulates risk-adjusted return.
- New product developments or business initiatives.
- Errors and omissions.

Trading desk:

- Detailed breakdown of all positions, including cash flows.
- Detailed P&L by portfolio and trader.
- Sensitivity modeling of all positions. This should include a sensitivity matrix indicating the vulnerability of the position to various changes in the variables affecting price.
- Compliance with limits.
- Errors and omissions.

– Product specific detail, such as contracts maturing or expiring, pertinent concentration information, etc.

Interest Rate Risk (Active Position-Takers and Limited End-Users)

The following discussion of interest rate risk applies to banks that use derivatives as active position-takers or limited end-users. Dealers, in addition to trading derivatives, can also be categorized as active position-takers or limited end-users when they use derivatives to manage interest rate risk in their treasury units.

Interest rate risk is the risk to earnings or capital arising from movements in interest rates. The economic (capital) perspective focuses on the value of the bank in today's interest rate environment and the sensitivity of that value to changes in interest rates. Interest rate risk arises from differences between the timing of rate changes and the timing of cash flows (repricing risk); from changing relationships among different yield curves affecting bank activities (basis risk); from changing rate relationships across the spectrum of maturities (yield curve risk); and from interest-related options embedded in bank products (options risk). The evaluation of interest rate risk must consider the impact of complex illiquid hedging strategies or products, and also the potential impact on fee income that is sensitive to changes in interest rates. When trading is separately managed, this impact is on structural positions rather than trading portfolios.

Banks are exposed to interest rate risk through their structural balance sheet positions. Banks using derivatives in an active position-taker or limited end-user capacity may do so:

- To limit downside earnings exposure.

- To preserve upside earnings potential.

- To increase return.

- To minimize income or economic value of equity (EVE) volatility.

The primary difference between an active position-taker/limited end-user and a dealer is that an end-user, rather than seeking to profit from short-term price movements, tries to manage its structural interest rate risk profile.

Both price and interest rate risk (e.g., changes in the term structure and volatility of interest rates) can be affected by many of the same variables. Hence there is overlap in the types of risk measurement systems, risk limits, and management information systems used for both. The primary differences in controls and MIS result from differences in the time horizons (shorter-term for dealers and longer-term for end-users) and the target accounts that management and the board focus on (trading revenue for dealers; earnings and the EVE for end-users).

Interest Rate Risk Management

Each institution using derivatives must establish an effective process for managing interest rate risk. The level of structure and formality in this process should be commensurate with the activities and level of risk approved by senior management and the board.

Contributing to effective supervision of interest rate risk are:

- Appropriate board and management supervision.

- Well-formulated policies and procedures.

- Reliable pricing and valuation systems.

- Accurate risk identification and measurement processes.

- Interest rate risk limits.

- Timely and effective risk reporting, monitoring, and exception approval processes.

Limited end-users and active position-takers are not expected to have the same degree of sophistication in their pricing systems as dealers. By definition, end-users are not quoting prices to customers. However, end-users must understand the factors affecting the price of derivatives to be able to effectively measure and manage potential risks to earnings and capital. In addition, end-users should have access to several pricing sources to ensure the reasonableness of the prices being quoted.

Because active position-takers use derivatives to alter their interest rate risk profile, they should have valuation and risk measurement systems comparable to the standards described for dealers (see the "Price Risk" section for more information). Limited end-users do not need the same sophisticated systems as those used by dealers or active position-takers. Nevertheless, they must be able to obtain market valuations and thoroughly assess the risks of the derivatives they hold. Independent third parties may be used for market values. However, any issues affecting independence (e.g., obtaining market values from the same dealer who sold the derivatives) need to be assessed by management and balanced against mitigating factors.

At a minimum, the risk measurement system (gap report, earnings, or EVE-at-risk analyses) should evaluate the possible impact on earnings and EVE (as applicable) that may result from adverse changes in interest rates and other market conditions. The measurement system should also allow management to monitor and evaluate the effectiveness of derivatives in the bank's overall interest rate risk profile. This system should include risk-adjusted return analyses.

Interest Rate Risk Measurement

Risk measurement systems should be able to identify and quantify in timely fashion the major sources of interest rate risk. The OCC expects all national banks to have systems that enable them to measure the amount of earnings-at-risk to changes in interest rates. Management at banks with significant medium- and long-term positions should be able to assess the longer-term impact of changes in interest rates on earnings and economic value of equity. The appropriate method of assessing longer-term exposures will depend upon the maturity and complexity of the bank's assets, liabilities, and off-balance-sheet activities. Methods range from gap reports that cover the full maturity range of the bank's activities to EVE measurement systems and simulation models.

There are a variety of ways to measure interest rate risk. The sophistication of an interest rate risk measurement system should be directly related to (1) the type and amount of interest rate risk, and (2) the ability of management to understand the nature, limitations, and meaning of the system's results. When a bank uses conservative limit structures in combination with conservative strategies, less sophisticated methodologies may be appropriate. For example, end-users with simple balance sheets and insignificant long-term positions may be able to manage interest rate risk with relatively basic techniques such as gap reports. However, banks with large or complex derivative activities should use more sophisticated measurement methods (such as earnings or EVE simulations). Regardless of the method for measuring and controlling interest rate risk, the board must be satisfied that effective controls are designed and implemented to limit the bank's vulnerability to interest rate risk.

Although they are generally more accurate, sophisticated interest rate risk measurement systems introduce the added risk that assumptions used in the model may not hold in all cases. Such a possibility is sometimes termed model risk. Banks should regularly re-evaluate interest rate risk model assumptions to ensure that they provide a reasonable estimate of risk for the scenarios being simulated. See the "Interest Rate Risk" section of the *Comptroller's Handbook* for more information on evaluating interest rate risk models.

At least annually, a summary of current interest rate risk measurement techniques and management practices should be provided to senior management and the board. This presentation should explicitly identify and report weaknesses or limiting assumptions in risk measurement models (e.g, an EAR simulation model may not identify longer-term exposures). Also, significant revisions to models should be reported and the impact on risk levels quantified.

Interest Rate Risk Limits

Interest rate risk limits should be commensurate with the level and type of interest rate exposure being taken. Standard limits used to control interest rate risk are described below.

Earnings and EVE-at-Risk Limits. These sensitivity limits are designed to restrict the amount of potential loss exposure. Active position-takers and limited end-users should be able to calculate the potential exposure of projected future reported earnings under varying interest rate scenarios. End-users with significant medium- and longer-term positions should also be able to assess the impact of changes in interest rates on EVE.

EAR and EVE-at-risk limits should reflect the quality of information and systems used in the risk measurement process. For instance, limited end-users who are capable of producing and analyzing only basic scenarios should establish conservative sensitivity limits.

EAR and EVE-at-risk limits are useful for controlling interest rate risk. However, the results are highly dependent upon the algorithms, assumptions, and methodology used by the model. Changes in any of these elements can produce widely different results. To address these issues, end-users should supplement these limits with other types of limits such as gap and notional limits.

Gap Limits. Gap (repricing) limits are designed to reduce loss exposure due to interest rate changes by controlling the volume of financial instruments that reprice or mature in a given time period.

Active position-takers and limited end-users may use gap limits to control the level and timing of their repricing imbalances. These limits are often expressed in terms of the ratio of rate-sensitive assets to rate-sensitive liabilities in a given time period. Such limits, however, do not readily convey the effect of repricing imbalances on future earnings. Limited end-users that rely on gap limits as their primary risk control tool should also determine the potential earnings exposure implied by these limits.

Notional or Volume Limits. Because notional limits do not provide a readily comparable proxy for interest rate risk, they are generally not acceptable by themselves. Nonetheless, limited end-users may use notional limits to control initial entry into derivative markets. Such limits may be satisfactory for banks holding very small volumes of plain-vanilla derivative products.

Management Information Systems

As mentioned earlier, the OCC believes that risk measurement and assessment should be conducted on an aggregate basis. The board and management should evaluate interest rate risk for the bank as a whole, in addition to consideration of other risks.

The following list includes standard reports needed to properly communicate interest rate risk. A bank's senior management and board or a board committee should receive reports on the bank's interest rate risk profile at least quarterly. More frequent reporting may be appropriate depending on the bank's level of risk and the potential that the level of risk could change significantly. The recipients of these reports may also vary depending on the bank's organizational structure.

- Board:

  - Current aggregate exposures as well as trends in aggregate interest rate risk.
  - Compliance with policies and risk limits.
  - Summary of performance relative to objectives that articulates risk-adjusted return (active position-takers).
  - Results of stress testing.
  - Summary of current risk measurement techniques and management practices (annually).

- Asset/Liability Management Committee or other executive management committee responsible for the supervision of interest rate risk:

  - Trends in exposure to interest rate risk.
  - Compliance with interest rate risk limits.
  - Summary of performance relative to objectives that articulates risk-adjusted return (active position-takers).
  - Major new product developments or business initiatives.
  - Results of stress testing, including major assumptions.
  - Summary of current risk measurement techniques and management practices (annually).

- Active position-takers will also need the following reports, as applicable.

  Business head/region:

  - Detailed profit and loss statement (P&L).
  - Summary of major exposures and offsets along with hedging alternatives.
  - Compliance with aggregate limits.
  - Summary of performance relative to objectives that articulates risk-adjusted return (active position-takers).
  - Major new product developments and business initiatives.
  - Results of stress testing, including major assumptions.

Liquidity Risk

Liquidity risk is the risk to earnings or capital from a bank's inability to meet its obligations when they come due, without incurring unacceptable losses. Liquidity risk includes the inability to manage unplanned decreases or changes in funding sources. Liquidity risk also arises from the failure to recognize or address changes in market conditions that affect the ability to liquidate assets quickly and with minimal loss in value. All institutions involved in derivatives face these two types of liquidity risk. For ease of discussion, these risks are referred to as funding liquidity risk and market liquidity risk. Controlling, measuring, and limiting both types of liquidity risk are vital activities and the sections that follow provide additional information on how to do so.

In developing guidelines for controlling liquidity risk, banks should consider the possibility of losing access to one or more markets, either because of concerns about their own creditworthiness, the creditworthiness of a major counterparty, or because of generally stressful market conditions. At such times, the bank may have less flexibility in managing its price, interest rate, credit, and liquidity risks. Banks that are market-makers in OTC derivatives or that dynamically hedge their positions require constant access to financial markets, and that need may increase in times of market stress. A bank's liquidity plan should consider its ability to access alternative markets, such as futures or cash markets, or to provide sufficient collateral or other credit enhancements in order to continue trading under a broad range of scenarios.

Risk management systems for liquidity risk are intertwined with those used in the management of price and interest rate risk. Consideration of market depth and the cash flow characteristics of particular instruments are critical in the establishment of risk limits and construction of portfolio stress tests. The management of price, interest rate, and liquidity risk is not conducted in isolation. As such, the examination of risk management systems for these three risks should be conducted concurrently.

Types of Liquidity Risk

Market Liquidity Risk

Market liquidity risk is the risk that a bank may not be able to exit or offset positions quickly, and in sufficient quantities, at a reasonable price. This inability may be due to inadequate market depth, market disruption, or the inability of the bank to access the market. Some bond and exotic product markets lack depth because of relatively fewer market participants. Even normally liquid markets can become illiquid during periods of market disruption (e.g., the stock market crash of October 1987, when there were more sellers than buyers). Market liquidity risk can also arise when a bank finds it difficult to access markets because of real or perceived credit or reputation problems of its own or of a major counterparty.

In dealer markets, the size of the bid/ask spread of a particular instrument provides a general indication of the market's depth. Market disruptions, a contraction in the number of market-markers, or the execution of large block transactions are some factors that may cause bid/ask spreads to widen.

Market disruptions may be limited or broad and can be created by a sudden and extreme imbalance in the supply and demand for products. In the OTC markets, the decision of only a few major market-makers to reduce participation in specific markets may decrease market liquidity, resulting in widening of the bid/ask spreads. The liquidity of certain markets may depend on the active presence of large institutional investors. If these investors pull out of the market or cease to trade actively, liquidity in the market will decline.

Market liquidity risk also involves the possibility that large transactions in particular instruments may have a significant effect on the transaction price. Large transactions can also strain liquidity in thin markets. An unexpected and sudden exit of market participants as a result of a sharp price movement or jump in volatility could lead to illiquid markets, and increased transaction costs, price, and interest rate risk.

Exchange-Traded Instruments. For exchange-traded instruments, counterparty credit exposures are assumed by the clearinghouse and managed through margin requirements and netting arrangements. The combination of margin requirements and netting arrangements is designed to limit the spread of credit and liquidity problems if individual participants have difficulty meeting their obligations. However, if there are sharp price changes in the market, margin calls can have adverse effects on liquidity. In such instances, market participants may find it necessary to sell assets to meet margin calls, further exacerbating any liquidity problems.

Many exchange-traded instruments are liquid only for small lots, and attempts to execute a large order can result in significant price changes. Additionally, not all contracts listed on the exchanges are actively traded. While some contracts have greater trading volume than the underlying cash markets, others trade infrequently. Even with actively traded futures or options contracts, the bulk of trading generally occurs in shorter-dated contracts. The volume of open interest in an exchange-traded contract is an indication of the liquidity of the contract.

OTC Instruments. Market liquidity in OTC dealer markets depends on the willingness of participants to accept the credit risk of major market-makers. Increases in the credit risk of one or more market-makers can significantly diminish the willingness of market participants to deal with these players, thereby adversely affecting liquidity. This factor particularly affects markets in which most activity is concentrated in a few market-makers.

Liquid secondary markets have developed for some OTC instruments. However, for most OTC derivatives, liquid secondary markets do not exist. Unlike cash and exchange-traded instruments, OTC contracts can be difficult to transfer or unwind because of their customized nature and relatively large contract size. In addition, OTC contracts generally can be canceled only by agreement with the other counterparty or through assignment of the contract(s), which can be difficult. As a result, dealers and active position-takers often manage these exposures by entering into another contract with similar but offsetting characteristics, or by using exchange-traded derivatives. Managing market exposures with offsetting contracts will reduce price risk, but will introduce additional counterparty credit risk.

Funding Liquidity Risk

Funding liquidity risk is the possibility that a bank may be unable to meet funding requirements at a reasonable cost. Such funding requirements arise each day from cash flow mismatches in swap books, the exercise of options, and the implementation of dynamic hedging strategies. The rapid growth of financial derivatives in recent years has focused increasing attention on the cash flow impact of such instruments.

Additional liquidity demands can result from collateral or margin calls and from early termination requests. Funding requirements can also result from adverse changes in the market's perception of the bank. Therefore, these issues should be incorporated into regular liquidity measurement, monitoring, and control processes.

Bank-specific weaknesses as well as systemic factors can impair the ability of a bank to access credit lines in the wholesale market. If the market perceives that the credit standing or reputation of the bank has deteriorated, customers may wish to reduce or eliminate their exposures to a bank by unwinding their in-the-money positions. Although the bank may not be contractually obligated to unwind positions, it may feel compelled to accommodate its counterparties if it perceives that refusal to do so would result in deterioration of a customer relationship or a further worsening of market perception. Similarly, the bank may have entered into credit-enhanced transactions containing margin and/or collateral provisions. Given these circumstances, the bank may be legally obligated to provide cash or cash-equivalent collateral to in-the-money counterparties. See the "Liquidity Risk Limit" and "Credit Risk Management Issues" sections for more information.

Liquidity Risk Management

The level of structure and formality in the liquidity risk management process should be commensurate with the activities and level of risk approved by senior management and the board. Liquidity risk is highest for dealers or active position-takers with significant unmatched derivative cash flows and significant foreign currency cash flows. These dealers and end-users should evaluate the cash flow impact of their off-balance-sheet activities in the context of the overall liquidity monitoring process. Tier II dealers and limited end-users with largely matched or relatively small positions may require less formal liquidity monitoring.

In dealer banks, market liquidity is controlled through price-risk-limit structures and risk management systems. Limits include restrictions on market participation, allowable tenors, and overall risk levels. In addition, the liquidity of markets and products should be considered when establishing the holding periods for price risk measurement. Management over these exposures should be monitored by the risk control function.

For dealers and active position-takers with significant unmatched positions or foreign currency cash flows, the supervision of day-to-day derivative cash flows should be a part of a bank's daily cash management process. Essential components for the proper control of liquidity risk include: open communication between line management and persons responsible for cash management; contingency liquidity plans; adequate measurement processes; limits controlling exposure to market illiquidity and mismatched cash flows; and comprehensive management information systems.

Communication

Managers responsible for derivatives and funding activities must regularly communicate market conditions to senior management. In turn, senior management must ensure that personnel are aware of any strategies or events that could affect market perception of the bank. Well-developed lines of communication, whether formal or informal, should be established between derivative managers and funding managers.

All banks with significant unmatched positions and foreign currency cash flows should provide funding managers with timely and adequate information regarding the volume and timing of these cash flows. This information should include, for example, any impending large transaction, such as an option exercise, swap payment, or foreign exchange settlement.
Tier II dealers and limited end-users with relatively few and simple transactions should also ensure good communication lines are in place between traders/risk-takers and liquidity management. However, they would generally not need to establish regular and formal management information systems because of the low volume of cash inflows and outflows.

Contingency Liquidity Planning

Deteriorating market liquidity has many symptoms: counterparties report they are full up and cannot transact further deals; prices are quoted at wider than normal market spreads; market participants increase demands for collateral or begin early termination agreements; or counterparties decline transactions in longer tenors. Such circumstances should trigger more cautious management of risk levels and may even require a bank to implement some of its contingency plans.

Contingency liquidity plans should address how price, interest rate, and market and funding liquidity risk would be managed if the bank's financial condition were to decline. Methods to control such exposure should be discussed, as well as specific strategies to reduce risk before counterparty lines become unavailable. The contingency plan should discuss the impact of credit enhancement agreements, any early termination triggers, expected funding needs, collateral requirements, management responsibilities, and action triggers to institute the plan. Management information systems should be able to supply quick and accurate information on derivative exposures to support this plan.

The contingency liquidity plan should identify authorized individuals and their responsibilities, circumstances that will trigger action, and alternative funding strategies for scenarios with successively deteriorating liquidity.

Liquidity Risk Measurement

Measurement of liquidity risk must include calculation of the liquidity impact of all significant on- and off-balance-sheet positions. The methods used to measure market liquidity risk should be similar in sophistication to those used in measuring price or interest rate risks. Particular care should be taken in evaluating and revising the amount of time it would take to exit or offset a position. Likewise, internal communication networks should enable the quick flow of market information.

Liquidity Risk Limits

In controlling liquidity risk, banks often place limits on tenor, open interest, payment mismatches, and notional or contract volumes. Banks should adopt reasonable holding periods. The initial and ongoing authorization to transact a product or to enter a market should ensure that the liquidity of those markets/products is commensurate with the bank's risk appetite. In addition, the bank's operating procedures should provide for early warning of potential liquidity concerns in the market.

Early Termination Agreements

The use of early termination agreements has grown in recent years as market participants have sought avenues to reduce counterparty credit exposure. However, the use of these agreements can be a double-edged sword. Although obtaining an early termination agreement from a counterparty can reduce a bank's credit risk, providing a counterparty with an early termination agreement can increase liquidity, price, and interest rate risk. Early terminations may be triggered when the bank can least afford the liquidity drain and the accompanying increase in price and interest rate risk (as trading or balance sheet hedge transactions are terminated, creating open positions). Management should enter into these agreements on a limited basis and only after careful consideration of their impact on price risk and liquidity exposures. The exposure resulting from such agreements should be tracked and fully incorporated into liquidity planning. In addition, bank policy should clearly define the circumstances, if any, under which management will honor a request for early termination when not contractually obligated.

Credit Enhancements

When the bank provides collateral to a counterparty, liquidity policies should define the maximum amount of assets that can be encumbered by collateral and margining arrangements, as well as the source of those assets. Limits should also be placed on the level of assets tied to collateral agreements with common triggers such as a credit rating threshold. The bank should carefully monitor and analyze the market environment and the potential collateral and margin demands under both current and adverse market conditions. The implications of these agreements should be formally incorporated into the bank's contingency funding plan. See the sections on credit, transaction, and compliance risk for more information.

Close-Out Reserves

Dealers using mid-market valuations should consider establishing valuation reserves to reflect the potential for market illiquidity upon closing out a position. In illiquid markets, bid/ask spreads can be wide and traders may find it difficult to close out a position at a reasonable cost. The potential additional cost of closing out the position would be reflected in the reserve. Close-out reserves may represent a significant portion of the mark-to-market exposure of a transaction or portfolio, especially for those transactions involving dynamic hedging. If a dealer elects to establish a close-out reserve, the reserve methodology should be documented and adjustments made as necessary. See the "Transaction Risk" section for more information on reserves.

Management Information Systems

MIS designed for liquidity measurement and monitoring should be commensurate with the bank's level of activity. Dealers and active position-takers with significant unmatched positions or foreign currency cash flows generally need the most sophisticated management information systems. Correspondingly, dealers with matched books, or end-users with low volume cash flows, generally need less sophisticated systems. For banks with significant cash flow mismatches or foreign currency settlements, MIS should also provide the capability of projecting cash flows under a variety of scenarios including: (1) a business as usual approach, which establishes the benchmark for the normal behavior of the bank's cash flows and (2) various liquidity crises.

At dealers with matched books and limited end-users with relatively few transactions, managers responsible for derivatives should provide funding managers with projections of the cash flows. These projections may be separate from or formally incorporated into standard cash flow gap reports. The format and timing should be sufficient to enable efficient management of cash flows.

Foreign Exchange Risk

Foreign exchange risk is the risk to earnings or capital arising from movement of foreign exchange rates. This risk is applicable to cross-border investing and operating activities. Market-making and position-taking in foreign currencies should be captured under price risk.

Foreign exchange risk is also known as translation risk. Foreign exchange translation risk arises from holding accrual accounts denominated in foreign currency, including loans, bonds, and deposits (i.e., cross-border investing). It also includes foreign-currency-denominated derivatives such as structured notes, synthetic investments, structured deposits, and off-balance-sheet derivatives used to hedge accrual exposures. Accounting conventions require periodic revaluation of these accounts at current exchange rates. This revaluation translates the foreign-denominated accounts into U.S. dollar terms. Banks should record these accrual-based products under appropriate systems that identify, measure, monitor, and control foreign exchange exposure.

The "Foreign Exchange" section of the *Comptroller's Handbook* may be useful to banks in managing this risk.

Credit Risk

Credit risk is the risk to earnings or capital of an obligor's failure to meet the terms of any contract with the bank or otherwise to perform as agreed. Credit risk arises from all activities in which success depends on counterparty, issuer, or borrower performance. It arises any time bank funds are extended, committed, invested, or otherwise exposed through actual or implied contractual agreements, whether reflected on or off the balance sheet.

Credit exposure arising from derivative activities should be addressed within the same framework used to assess credit risk in traditional banking activities. Counterparty credit risk can be effectively managed through accurate measurement of exposures, ongoing monitoring, timely counterparty credit evaluations, and sound operating procedures. In addition, there are a growing number of mechanisms that can reduce credit exposure, such as netting arrangements, credit enhancements, and early termination agreements.

Types of Credit Risk

Credit risk in derivative products comes in the form of pre-settlement risk and settlement risk.

Pre-settlement risk is the risk of loss due to a counterparty defaulting on a contract during the life of a transaction. Presettlement exposure consists of both current exposure (the replacement cost of the derivative transaction or its market value) and the add-on (an estimate of the future replacement cost of the derivative).

Calculating presettlement risk is more complex than assessing the credit risk of traditional lending products. The maximum credit exposure from traditional banking activities is generally limited to the amount of funds advanced or invested at the time of a customer default. For many off-balance-sheet derivatives, however, there is no advancement of funds or exchange of principal. Therefore, the risk of loss is conditional on the counterparty defaulting AND the derivative contract having positive value to the bank (an in-the-money contract) at the time of default. The level of this exposure varies throughout the life of the derivative contract. Even derivative contracts that are out-of-the-money (i.e., contracts where the bank has no current loss exposure because the mark-to-market is positive for the counterparty, not the bank) have potential credit risk, because changes in market factors can cause the value of the contract to become positive to the bank at any point prior to maturity. To manage credit risk effectively, a bank should develop a reliable method of estimating potential credit exposure.

Settlement risk is the loss exposure arising when a bank meets its obligation under a contract before the counterparty meets its obligation. A failure to perform may be due to counterparty default, operational breakdown, or legal impediments.

Settlement risk lasts from the time an outgoing payment instruction can no longer be canceled unilaterally until the time the incoming payment is received with finality and reconciled. This risk arises because it is generally impractical to arrange simultaneous payment and delivery in the ordinary course of business. For example, settlement risk arises in international transactions because of time zone differences. This risk generally exists for a minimum of one to two days. It can take another one to two business days to confirm receipt through reconciliation procedures. As a result, settlement risk can often last more than three business days before a bank can be certain that a payment has been received. Depending on the delivery process for the instrument, settlement risk is usually greater than pre-settlement risk on any given transaction. Banks should monitor and control settlement risk separately from pre-settlement risk.

Senior managers as well as sales, trading, operations, risk control, and credit management should understand the settlement process and be aware of the timing of key events in the process, when payment instructions are recorded, when they become irrevocable, and when confirmation of counterparty payment is received with finality. Knowledge of these items allows the duration and value of settlement exposure to be better quantified and controlled.

Credit Risk Management

Each institution must have an effective means of measuring and controlling derivatives credit risk. Examiners need to know whether the bank is a dealer or end-user and whether risk controls are appropriate. A prudently controlled environment will include the following:

- Effective senior management and board oversight.

- Policies and procedures.

- Strong credit review, approval, and limit processes.

- Accurate and validated risk measurement systems.

- Timely and effective risk reporting, monitoring, and exception approval processes.

- Proper credit documentation standards.

Counterparty credit risk should be strictly controlled through a formal and independent credit process. Credit activities must be guided by policies and procedures. To alleviate conflicts of interest, the credit approval function should be independent of the risk-taking unit and staffed by qualified personnel. Independence must be maintained for the initial credit assessment, establishment of counterparty credit lines, monitoring and reporting of exposure, and approval of exceptions. These functions are typically performed by the bank's credit division.

In order to effectively evaluate risk exposure and set appropriate credit limits, the personnel responsible for approving and monitoring credit exposure (e.g., relationship officers and loan review) must possess a basic understanding of derivative instruments, the source of credit exposure, and market factors that affect credit exposure. Credit personnel should receive ongoing training on derivative instruments, risk management techniques, and methods of measuring credit risk.

The credit department should periodically review the creditworthiness of derivative counterparties and assign risk ratings to them, as they would to customers buying traditional bank products. Good communication between the risk-taking unit and credit department are essential to ensure that all parties are informed of a change in the credit line or creditworthiness of a counterparty. Nonperforming contracts should be reported consistent with the bank's internal policy for nonperforming loans. The quality of derivative counterparty portfolio and the integrity of risk ratings should be periodically reviewed by the loan review function (or similar independent party).

Credit Reserves

Dealers or end-users with significant derivative activity should maintain credit reserves for counterparty credit exposure. According to generally accepted accounting principles (GAAP), the allowance established for derivative credit exposure should be maintained separate from the allowance for loan and lease losses. Credit reserves should reflect the exposure adjusted for the probability of default. Ideally, it should be based on actual and potential exposures to counterparties (taking into account legally enforceable netting arrangements), estimated default rates over the life of the transactions, collateral arrangements, and recovery rates. As the current replacement costs and potential exposures change through time, the reserve should be adjusted. See the "Transaction Risk" section for additional information on reserves.

Customer Appropriateness

Derivative dealers must also establish controls that assess the appropriateness of specific transactions for customers. These controls are necessary to manage credit and reputation risk to the bank. A customer that engages in a transaction that it does not understand, is inconsistent with its policies, or is otherwise inappropriate, poses a credit risk because that customer may be unable to anticipate the risks these obligations entail. If that customer defaults, there is a greater potential for litigation and damage to the bank's reputation.

To ensure customer appropriateness, dealer banks need to understand the nature of each counterparty's business and the purpose of its derivative activities. The same level of knowledge about a customer as that required for traditional lending transactions is needed, and this understanding should be documented in the credit file.

For customers considered to be dealers or sophisticated end-users, it is sufficient to note that these are market professionals who will be using derivative products for market-making or risk management purposes. For less sophisticated customers, dealers need to attempt to understand the particular risk that a customer is trying to manage and ascertain whether the derivative product under consideration is an appropriate tool for that customer. Usual and customary credit file information, including the customer's risk profile, business characteristics and plans, financial statements, and the type and purpose of credit facilities, should be sufficient to evaluate appropriateness.

These appropriateness standards do not require banks to obtain and review counterparties' policies or verify the data the counterparties used to identify and assess the risks they are seeking to manage. However, some transactions, by reason of their type, size, structure, or risk characteristics, may require the approval of the counterparty's senior management.

Consistent with safe and sound banking practices, the bank should not recommend transactions that management knows, or has reason to believe, are inappropriate for a customer. Similarly, if the bank believes that a customer does not understand the risks of a derivative transaction, the bank should consider refraining from the transaction. If the customer wishes to proceed, bank management should document its analysis of the transaction and any risk disclosure information provided to the customer.

Some banks have adopted standardized risk disclosure statements to inform counterparties of the major risks of a derivative transaction and to clarify the counterparty's relationship with the bank. These statements may be useful in educating counterparties about the bank's view of the relationship; however, courts may look beyond the standard statement in evaluating the nature of the relationship between the parties. Therefore, banks should not rely unduly on these statements to protect them from liability, but should continually assess the true character of the relationship with the counterparty.

Transactions with Undisclosed Counterparties

Growth in the managed funds business has led to increased demand by agents and advisors that banks enter into sizeable transactions with undisclosed counterparties. By not disclosing the principals to these trades, agents and advisors hope to preserve client confidentiality, minimize client poaching, and increase transaction efficiency by entering into block trades. For competitive reasons, some commercial banks feel compelled to enter into such transactions after they establish controls.

Dealing with undisclosed counterparties involves significant credit, compliance, and reputation risks. Accordingly, only banks with well constructed risk management systems should engage in such transactions. If a bank desires to engage in these activities, the associated risks must be carefully studied by senior management *and* the board. If the bank chooses to engage in transactions with undisclosed counterparties, exposures should be carefully controlled and monitored. Controls that a bank should establish include:

- Restricting transactions with agents and other intermediaries to persons and firms who are reputable and who agree to the bank's risk management requirements.

- Requiring agents and other intermediaries to restrict transactions with the bank to an approved list of counterparties with predesignated credit limits for each permissible counterparty.

- Limiting the size of transactions with agents and other intermediaries acting on behalf of undisclosed counterparties both individually and in aggregate.

- Limiting transactions to liquid spot or short-term forward foreign exchange transactions, or high-quality securities with regular way delivery versus payment (DVP) settlement.

- Requiring third-party guarantees or collateral to ensure performance, wherever feasible.

Because undisclosed counterparty transactions may create uncertainty about whether liability rests with the agent/intermediary or the principal, legal opinions should be obtained concerning the enforceability of any written agreements. Legal opinions should also be sought on ensuring compliance with money laundering statutes. See the "Compliance Risk" section for more information.

Credit Risk Measurement

Presettlement Risk

Banks should have a system to quantify pre-settlement risk. Pre-settlement credit risk can be estimated using a variety of methods. Techniques have evolved from using the full notional amount of the contract, to a percentage of the notional amount, to loan equivalent estimates. Many banks now employ highly sophisticated computer models to simulate the potential credit exposure over the life of a derivative contract.

The credit risk in a derivative product is a function of several factors. The risk depends on the type of contract, cash flows, price volatility, tenor, etc. Exposure at the beginning of a contract is usually at or near zero. Most deals are done at market prices (off-market deals create an immediate credit exposure, with the risk most often taken by the bank), and most derivative contracts do not involve an exchange of principal. After inception, the expected risk increases or decreases to reflect the impact of changing price factors. The longer the contract, the greater the potential for rate movements and, hence, a change in potential exposure. Credit risk is generally reduced over the life of the contract because (1) interim cash flows reduce payment uncertainty and (2) the shorter the remaining life of the contract the less potential there is that significant adverse rate movements will occur. The credit exposure will often be skewed to either the beginning or the end of the contract depending on the size of the rate differentials and timing of cash flows.

The method used to measure counterparty credit risk should be commensurate with the volume and level of complexity of the derivative activity. Dealers and active position-takers should have access to statistically calculated loan-equivalent exposures, which represent the current exposure (replacement cost) plus an estimate of the potential change in value over the remaining life of the contract (add-on). The replacement cost calculation simply involves marking-to-market each derivative contract. The add-on is generally determined using model-based simulation. When modeling price risk, a bank should use a holding period that reflects how long it would take to offset or close out a position. However, when modeling the credit risk add-on, a bank should make the time horizon the remaining life of the contract, because default can occur at any time. More information on credit risk add-ons can be found in appendix H.

Limited end-users may elect to use a less sophisticated method for measuring the credit risk add-on (e.g., a percent of notional value times number of remaining years to maturity) as long as they take other mitigating actions. Such actions include restricting transactions to the highest quality counterparties and limiting activities to mature, less volatile derivative contracts.

Credit enhancements and close-out netting arrangements also affect the calculated level of credit exposure. If the bank has a valid security interest or lien on marketable assets or cash, the level of credit exposure reported for that counterparty may be reduced commensurately (or at least identified as a separate line item).

Settlement Risk

Settlement risk exposure is the cumulative amount of funds or assets delivered for payment and lasts from the time an outgoing payment order can no longer be canceled unilaterally, until the time the incoming payment is received with finality and reconciled. The duration of an individual bank's settlement exposure will depend on the characteristics of the relevant payments systems as well as on the bank's internal reconciliation procedures.

Settlement practices can create interbank exposures that last several days. This is particularly true of transactions settling across time zones. Given current industry practices, a bank's maximum settlement exposure could equal, or even surpass, the amount receivable for three days' worth of trades, so that at any point in time, the amount at risk to even a single counterparty could exceed a bank's capital. FX transactions, in particular, involve a higher degree of settlement risk because the full notional value is exchanged. It is not uncommon for larger dealer banks to settle FX trades worth well over
$1 billion with a single counterparty on a single day.

Banks can reduce settlement exposure by negotiating their correspondent arrangements to reduce the amount of time they are exposed to non-cancelable payments awaiting settlement. Further, banks should review the time necessary for reconciliation of payment receipt. Reducing the time it takes to identify final and failed trades will reduce settlement exposure.

Banks should also net settlement payments, when legally permissible, rather than settling on a trade-by-trade basis. Netting is discussed later in this section, in appendix I, and in the "Transaction Risk" and "Compliance Risk" sections.

Credit Risk Limits

Counterparty credit limits should be approved before the execution of derivative transactions. Banks should establish counterparty credit limits in much the same way as traditional credit lines. Documentation in the credit file should support the purpose, payment source, and collateral (if any). Evaluations of individual counterparty credit limits should aggregate limits for derivatives with the credit limits established for other activities, including commercial lending.

Presettlement risk limits should be established that are commensurate with the board's risk tolerance and the sophistication of the bank's risk measurement system. Less precise credit risk measures should be supplemented with more conservative limits. For example, limited end-users commonly use percent of notional amount for measuring credit risk. However, such banks should establish conservative presettlement risk limits that take into consideration the imprecision of these measures.

Banks should have distinct limits for settlement risk. The dollar volume of exposure due to settlement risk is often greater than the credit exposure arising from presettlement risk because settlement risk sometimes involves exchange of the total notional value of the instrument or principal cash flow. However, it is important to understand that settlement risk exists only when principal cash flows are exchanged and delivery versus payment is not applied. Limits should reflect the credit quality of the counterparty and the bank's own capital adequacy, operations efficiency, and credit expertise. Any transaction that will exceed a limit should be pre-approved by an appropriate credit officer. Reports to managers should enable them to easily recognize limits that have been exceeded.

Mechanisms to Reduce Credit Exposure

A number of mechanisms can reduce credit exposure, including netting arrangements, credit enhancements, and early termination agreements. In recent years, banks have increasingly used these tools not only to reduce credit exposure but also to minimize transaction costs and manage credit lines more efficiently.

Before recognizing the reduction in credit risk that these arrangements provide, banks must ensure that they are properly documented and legally enforceable. Terms of these arrangements are usually outlined in a standardized master agreement covering specific products such as the International Swaps and Derivatives Association (ISDA) agreement, Foreign Exchange and Options Agreement (FEOMA), and International Currency Options Market (ICOM) agreement. Banks must also ensure that the arrangements are legally enforceable in the relevant jurisdictions. See the "Compliance Risk" section for more information on documentation and enforceability. Finally, banks must ensure that they have adequate operational capacity to perform the necessary calculations or otherwise accommodate these arrangements.

Additional information regarding netting, credit enhancements, and early termination agreements may be found in the "Transaction Risk" and "Compliance Risk" sections and appendices I, J, and K.

Management Information Systems

Risk measurement and assessment should be conducted on an aggregate basis. When evaluating derivative credit risk, bank management should consider this exposure in the context of the bank's total credit exposure to the counterparty.

Management reports need to communicate effectively the nature of counterparty activities. Reports should be tailored to the intended audience. These reports will often cover the same subject, but the level of detail will vary depending on the recipient. Reports should be meaningful, timely, and accurate. They should be generated from sources independent of the dealing function, and distributed to all appropriate levels of management. The recipients of these reports may vary depending on the bank's organizational structure.

Daily reports should, at a minimum, address significant counterparty line usage and limit exceptions. Banks should be able to combine the loan-equivalent figures with other credit risks to determine the aggregate risk for each counterparty. Monthly reports should detail portfolio information on industry concentrations, tenors, exception trends, and other relevant information with respect to pre-settlement exposure.

For dealers, active-position takers, and high volume limited end-users, credit exposure reports should include the following types of information.

- Board:

  - Trends in overall counterparty credit risk.
  - Compliance with policies, procedures, and counterparty limits.

- Credit or Executive Committee:

  - Trends in counterparty credit risk.
  - Concentrations.
  - Credit reserve summary.
  - Compliance with policies, procedures, and counterparty limits.
  - Trends in credit exceptions.
  - Periodic reports on credit risk model development and model validation reviews.

- Business head:

  - Trends in counterparty credit risk. Should include trends in risk ratings and nonperforming accounts. Exposure can be reported, as appropriate, on a gross mark-to-market, net mark-to-market, peak, or average exposure basis.
  - Concentrations. Should consider both external and internal factors. External factors include countries, regions, and industries. Internal factors include major counterparty exposure, tenors, and risk ratings.
  - Credit reserve summary.
  - Compliance with policies and procedures. Should detail exceptions, their frequency and trends.
  - Aggregate exposure versus limits. May include actual exposure as a percentage of limits.
  - Trends in credit limit and documentation exceptions. Should include status and trends of past-due counterparty reviews, progress in formalizing standard industry agreements, progress

in formalizing netting agreements, and status of other credit-related exceptions.
- Periodic reports on credit risk model development. Should include independent certifications and periodic validations of the models.

- Dealing room and desk, as applicable:

  - Detail of counterparty lines and credit availability, including a "watch" list of counterparties that are approaching limits.
  - Compliance with limits.
  - Errors and omissions.

Transaction Risk

Transaction risk is the risk to earnings or capital arising from problems with service or product delivery. This risk is a function of internal controls, information systems, employee integrity, and operating processes. Transaction risk exists in all products and services. Derivative activities can pose challenging operational risks because of their complexity and continual evolution. The operations function, which is discussed in a later section, refers to the product support systems and related processes.

As part of their fiduciary responsibility, the board and senior management must institute a sound internal control framework to prevent losses caused by fraud and human error. Fundamental to this framework is the segregation of the operations and risk-taking functions. Many well publicized financial mishaps (e.g., the Barings Bank, Daiwa Bank, and Sumitomo Corporation) have illustrated the peril of failing to segregate key risk-taking and operational functions.

Adequate systems and sufficient operational capacity are essential to support derivative activities. This is especially true for dealers and active position-takers who process large volumes of transactions daily. Just as trading systems have evolved, operational systems must keep pace with the rapid growth in both the volume and complexity of derivatives products. In today's fast-paced environment, trades must be processed quickly not only to service the counterparty but also to update position management and credit line monitoring systems.

Skilled and experienced staff are integral to the efficient operation of back office systems. This is especially true for derivatives activities because of their complex nature. Management should regularly determine whether the staff members processing derivatives transactions have the knowledge and skills necessary for the job and whether their numbers are sufficient.

Banks should not participate in derivative activities if their systems, operations, personnel, or internal controls are not sufficient to support the management of transaction risk.

Transaction Risk Management

In order to effectively manage transaction risk, senior managers must fully understand the processing cycle and must change processes and technology when necessary. They should identify areas of transaction risk and estimate the loss a bank could suffer from a given exposure.

To minimize transaction risk and ensure efficient processing, all personnel involved in derivatives activities should understand the differing roles played by sales, trading, risk control, credit, operations, and accounting. Operations personnel cannot adequately support a business activity they do not understand. Insufficient knowledge of derivatives prevents an understanding of the risks involved and may prevent effective internal controls from being implemented. The operations unit needs to evolve from a clerical processing room into a professional, value-adding division that is competent in derivative products. The staff must be self-reliant, knowledgeable of derivative products, and have technical abilities that enable them to communicate and work effectively with front office traders. Accordingly, a bank should provide back-office personnel with appropriate continuing education.

The degree of sophistication in an operations system should be commensurate with the level of risk. For derivative dealers and active position-takers, a system with extensive capabilities is generally needed to efficiently process, confirm, and record transaction details. Limited end-users may use a personal computer with spreadsheets or other devices to record transaction data. Regardless of the type of support system used, certain fundamental requirements for the processing and control functions remain the same. These requirements are discussed later in this section.

Weak operational processes increase the possibility of loss from human error, fraud, or systems failure. Operational errors may affect the accuracy of management reports and risk measurement systems, thus jeopardizing the quality of management decisions. For example, losses can occur not only from settlement errors but also from managing incorrect positions or misstating credit exposure because trade data was input incorrectly. Further, operational errors and inefficiencies can harm a bank's reputation and cause a loss of business.

A properly controlled transaction risk management function should include:

- Effective board and senior management supervision.

- Policies and procedures.

- Segregation of risk-taking and operational duties.

- Skilled and experienced operations personnel.

- Timely financial, exposure, and risk reporting (as applicable).

- Operational performance measures.

- Technology commensurate with the level and complexity of activity.

Transaction Risk Measurement

The level of transaction risk associated with a bank's derivative activities is related to (1) the volume and complexity of transactions and (2) the efficiency and integrity of the operations department. The better the bank's ability to prevent losses from human error, fraud, and weak operational systems, the lower will be the level of transaction risk.

One way to measure transaction risk is to monitor the quality and efficiency of operations vis-a-vis quantifiable performance measures. This is particularly important for dealers transacting large volumes of trades. Examples of operating performance measures include the number of transactions processed per employee and overtime hours worked. Other examples of performance measures include: the volume of disputed, unconfirmed, or failed trades; reconciling items; and documentation exceptions. Timeframes for resolving discrepancies should be documented, evaluated, and regularly reported to senior management.

Role of Operations

The function of an operations department is to process transactions, record contracts, and reconcile transactions and databases. A properly functioning operations department will help ensure the integrity of financial information and minimize operations, settlement, and legal risks. The operations area should provide the necessary checks to detect unauthorized trades.

Typically, the dealing/risk-taking and sales functions are referred to as the *front office* and the processing and recording/reporting areas are referred to as the *back office*. In some banks, a *middle office* helps reconcile systems, monitor positions and revenues, and perform related activities. Banks create middle offices to be able to calculate and verify profits and losses, as well as position risk, in a more timely fashion. Like the back office, the middle office should operate independently of the risk-taking environment.

At banks for which establishing a separate risk control unit is not economical, the back office will generally be responsible for much of the risk control. This may include exposure/position reporting, monitoring of credit and price limits, and profit and loss reporting.

Transaction risk is very difficult to quantify. The ability to control this risk depends on accurate transaction updates to all systems (e.g., trading, settlement, credit, and general ledger). Back-office personnel, who are responsible for accounting records, confirmations, reconciliation and settlement, must maintain a reporting line independent of front-office personnel. On-line credit systems should calculate aggregate exposure globally with credit exposure and credit usage information updated as soon as deals are transacted. Procedures should be established to segregate duties among persons responsible for: making investment and credit decisions; confirmations; recordkeeping; reconciliations; and disbursing and receiving funds.

Policies and Procedures

Policies and procedures are the framework for managing transaction risk. Banks should insure that operating policies and procedures are developed and regularly updated. Procedures manuals can take different forms, but their detail should be commensurate with the nature of derivative activities. Policies and procedures for derivatives activities need not be stand-alone documents, but rather can be incorporated into other applicable policies such as operations guidance on interest rate risk, investment securities, and dealing activities. The documents should guide employees through the range of tasks performed and should contain guidance on relevant areas of trade processing, account valuations, reconciliations, and documentation.

The following issues should be addressed in policies and procedures.

Trade Capture

In the front office, the risk-taker transacts a deal directly over a recorded phone line, through a broker, or through an electronic matching system. After the deal is executed, the risk-taker or operations staff should immediately input trade data into the trading system (or write a ticket to be entered into a bank's operations system). Information on deals transacted over electronic dealing systems can flow electronically to update relevant reports and databases. All trades should be entered promptly so that all systems can be updated (e.g., credit, intra-day P&L, risk positions, confirmation processing, settlement, and general ledger).

Trade information captured includes trade date, time of trade, settlement date, counterparty, financial instrument traded and amount transacted, price or rate, and netting instructions. Settlement instructions sometimes accompany this information. The trading system uses this information to update position and P&L reports or on-line systems. Deal information captured by trading system may also flow into the credit system so that settlement and presettlement exposures can be updated.

Ideally, the front-office system should have one-time data capture for transactions to maximize operational efficiency. That is, after the trade is executed, the system should automatically generate accounting entries, confirmations, update trader positions, credit risk exposure reports, and other relevant databases. One-time data capture can significantly minimize the possibility of subsequent data entry errors at the manual level.

Confirmation Process

The purpose of the confirmation process is to verify that each derivative counterparty agrees to the terms of the trade. For each trade, a confirmation is issued by the bank, and the counterparty either issues its own confirmation or affirms the bank's confirmation. To reduce the likelihood of fraud or human error, this confirmation process must be conducted independently of the risk-taking unit.

To minimize risk, a bank should make every effort to send confirmations within one to three hours after deals are executed and no later than the end of the business day. Inefficient confirmation issuance and receipt make it difficult to detect errors that may lead to problems in P&L reconciliation and position valuation.

The method of confirmation varies depending on the type of counterparty, derivative traded, and the method of settlement. Ideally, confirmations are exchanged electronically with the counterparty via the Society for Worldwide Interbank Financial Telecommunications (SWIFT) or an electronic matching service.

Although phone confirmations can help to reduce the number and size of trade discrepancies, they are no substitute for physical confirmations. Except when contracts have very short maturities, it is poor practice to rely solely on telephone verifications. Errors may be made in interpreting terminology used over the phone. In addition, certain jurisdictions only recognize physical confirmations for litigation purposes.

Unconfirmed and Disputed Trades

All incoming confirmations should be sent to the attention of a department that is independent of the risk-taking unit. Incoming information should be compared with the outgoing confirmation, and any disputes should be carefully researched. Disputes or unconfirmed trades should be brought immediately to the attention of the operations manager. All disputes and unconfirmed trades should be regularly reported to a senior operations officer.

A bank should adopt standard procedures for addressing disputes and unconfirmed deals. Documentation should include the key financial terms of the transaction, indicate the disputed item, and summarize the resolution. The counterparty should receive notice of the final disposition of the trade and an adequate audit trail of the notice should be on file in the back office. Risk-taking and sales personnel should be notified of disputed or unconfirmed deals.

Netting

Netting is an agreement between counterparties to offset positions or obligations. Payment (or settlement) netting is a bilateral (two-party) agreement intended to reduce settlement risk. Payment netting is a mechanism in which parties agree to net payments payable between them on any date, in the same currency, under the same transaction or a specified group of transactions. Payment netting goes on continually during the life of a master agreement. Payment netting reduces credit and transaction risk by allowing the bank to make one payment instead of settling multiple transactions individually. However, a bank should not perform payment netting without first ensuring that netting agreements are properly documented and legally enforceable. Banks often use standardized master agreements such as the International Swaps and Derivatives Association (ISDA) agreement, Foreign Exchange and Options Agreement (FEOMA), and International Currency Options Market (ICOM) agreement to document netting arrangements. The credit and compliance risk aspects of netting are discussed in their respective sections.

Despite the obvious advantages of netting, it presents operational complexities and its use is mainly confined to the largest banks and counterparties. Banks cite costs and lack of operational capacity, as well as legal uncertainties, as barriers to the greater use of netting arrangements. Banks performing netting should ensure that they have the systems to accurately and quickly calculate net payments. Correct calculations of netted payments are important to preserve counterparty relationships and avoid costly errors. Some banks use payment netting services such as FXNET, SWIFT, and VALUNET to calculate net payments. These on-line systems allow counterparties to communicate directly with each other and avoid costly discrepancies. Some pairs of banks have set up bilateral netting arrangements on their own using standardized netting contracts. Additional information on bilateral netting can be found in the "Compliance Risk" section and appendix I.

Banks can reduce credit and transaction exposure by using multilateral netting arrangements. Multilateral netting is designed to extend the benefits of bilateral netting to cover contracts with a group of counterparties. Often, under a multilateral netting arrangement, a clearinghouse interposes itself as the legal counterparty for covered contracts transacted between its members. The most familiar form of multilateral netting is in the clearing and settlement of contracts on futures and options exchanges. There are also multilateral clearinghouses for OTC foreign exchange transactions operating in the United States and the United Kingdom. Additional information on multilateral netting can be found in the "Compliance Risk" section and appendix I.

Management should confirm that operational procedures ensure that netting is carried out as contractually obligated between a bank and its counterparties. Operations should ensure that netted trades are reflected in trade capture systems and credit systems so that netting is successfully executed. The operational procedures should include any necessary cut-off times, settlement instructions, and the method of confirmation/affirmation and should be supported by the documentation of the counterparty.

Settlement Process

Settlement refers to the process through which trades are cleared by the payment/receipt of currency, securities, or cash flows on periodic payment dates and the date of final settlement. The settlement of derivative transactions can involve the use of various international and domestic payment system networks.

By separating the duties of operations staff members, a bank asserts vital control over the settlement process. Like other operations functions, the settlement process should be controlled through procedures directing the payment/receipt of funds. Specifically, operations procedures should address regular terms of settlement, exception processes, and the reporting of stale-dated or unusually large unsettled transactions. The person(s) responsible for the release of funds should be independent of the confirmation process as well as areas of transaction processing that could allow access to the payment process. Such sensitive areas include, for instance, access to standardized settlement instructions.

Because failed trades or unsettled items increase settlement risk and cause inaccuracies in P&L, position, and credit reporting, they should be identified and resolved as soon as possible. Anything more than a routine situation should be brought to the attention of risk-taking management and the senior operations officer.

Reconciliations

To ensure that data has been accurately captured, critical data points and reports should be promptly reconciled. The person who reconciles accounts must be independent of the person who initiates the transaction or inputs transaction data. The general ledger should be reconciled with front and back systems each day. Front and back office P&L and position reports should also be reconciled each day. Regulatory reports should be periodically reconciled to the general ledger. Reconcilement discrepancies should be investigated and resolved as soon as possible. Significant discrepancies should be brought to the attention of senior management.

Broker's Commissions and Fees

The back office should review brokers' statements, reconcile charges to bank estimates and the general ledger, check commissions, and initiate payment. Brokers should be approved independently of the risk-takers. The back office should monitor brokerage activity to ensure that it is conducted with only approved brokers and that trades are distributed to a reasonable number of brokers. Unusual trends or charges should be brought to the attention of back office management and reviewed with the appropriate personnel.

Documentation and Record-Keeping

Transaction documentation for derivative instruments often requires written confirmation of trades, contract terms, legal authorities, etc. Typically, many of the terms under which the instruments are transacted are stipulated in master agreements and other legal documents. Maintaining proper documentation and ensuring proper completion and receipt is often the responsibility of the operations or credit functions. Banks should establish processes (checklists, tickler files, etc.) to ensure that derivative transactions, like all other risk-taking transactions, are properly documented. These processes should monitor and control receipt of documents. Banks should establish thresholds limiting future business with counterparties failing to provide required documentation. Proper control over derivative documentation requires a process that quickly identifies and resolves documentation exceptions. The role of legal counsel in the documentation process is discussed in the "Compliance Risk" section.

Revaluation Approaches and Reserves

Both the risk control and audit functions should ensure that position valuations are generated from independent sources. Accurate values are key to the generation of reliable reports on risk levels, profitability, and trends. Ideally, much of the valuation process employs valuation model algorithms or electronic data feeds from wire services, with little manual intervention. When reliable revaluation models or data feeds are not available, as is the case with some illiquid or highly customized products, operations personnel or other independent personnel should obtain values from other dealers or use approved mathematical techniques to derive values.

The process through which positions are marked-to-market should be specified in policies and procedures. Controls should be implemented that ensure proper segregation of duties between risk-takers and control personnel, including the independent input and verification of market rates. In addition, controls should provide for consistent use of pricing methods and assumptions about pricing factors (e.g., volatility) to ensure accurate financial reporting and consistent evaluations of price risk.

The approach banks use to value their derivative portfolios will depend on a variety of factors including the liquidity and complexity of the contracts and the sophistication of their valuation and accounting systems. The most conservative approach is using the bid for long positions and the offer for short positions. Some dealers will take a conservative approach with illiquid or highly structured derivative portfolios by valuing them at the lower of cost or market (LOCOM).

Dealers and more sophisticated end-users typically value transactions at mid-market less adjustments (usually through the use of reserves) for future costs. The most common types of adjustments are those made to reflect credit risk and future administrative costs. Other types of adjustments may be made to reflect close-out costs, investing and funding costs, and costs associated with valuation model errors. At a minimum, banks using mid-market valuations should make adjustments for credit risk and administrative costs. If a bank elects not to use adjustments for close-out costs, investment and funding costs, and model errors, its rationale should be documented.

Regardless of the valuation method used, management should ensure that policies and procedures are established that support their valuation. If mid-market less adjustments is used, policies and procedures should specify required valuation adjustments, documentation of valuation rationale, periodic review of assumptions, and appropriate accounting treatment.

Dealers should mark positions to market at least daily (intraday marks may be necessary in some market environments) and on an official, independent basis, no less frequently than once a month. For risk management purposes, active position-takers should independently revalue derivative positions at least once a month and should possess the ability to obtain reliable market values daily if warranted by market conditions. Limited end-users should establish a time frame for revaluations that is consistent with other risk measurements. At a minimum, revaluations should be conducted by end-users at least quarterly.

Although independent revaluation of exchange-traded instruments is readily accomplished through published contract prices, the valuation of less actively transacted instruments, particularly the less liquid and more exotic OTC derivatives, is more difficult. Certain volatility rates and other parameters can be difficult to generate without input from the risk-taker. However, if a bank wishes to deal in or use these products, it must have a mechanism to independently and consistently derive needed market rates from similar markets or other dealers.

In obtaining external valuations, the requirements of the valuation should be specified (for example: mid, bid, offer, indicative, firm). In addition, when external valuations are received they should be considered in light of the relationship with the party supplying them and, in particular, whether they include factors that may make them inappropriate (for example, obtaining valuations from the originating dealer).

The revaluation process should include a review of trades executed at off-market rates. These trades may result from human error or undesirable trader or counterparty activity. A daily procedure should be followed that provides for an independent review, whether manual or automated, of trade prices relative to prevailing market rates. Any deals conducted at off-market rates should be reported to the senior operations and risk-taking management and risk control.

Procedures for documenting and resolving discrepancies between front office inputs and back office inputs should be firmly established. Documentation containing the reason for the discrepancy, the profit and loss impact, and the final resolution of the discrepancy should be maintained. Significant discrepancies should be reported to senior operations and risk-taking management. Independence in establishing revaluation information should not be compromised.

Information Technology

Although systems and modeling technology supports a derivatives business, technology can also pose significant risks.

The degree of sophistication of systems technology should be commensurate with the character and complexity of the derivatives business. In assessing risk, management and the board should consider how well the management information system functions, rather than its technical specifications. The system should serve the needs of applicable users, including senior management, risk control units, front office, back office, financial reporting, and internal audit. For large systems, the bank should have flow charts or other documentation that show data flow from input through reporting.

An important aspect in the evaluation of information technology is how well different systems interface. (Interface is usually accomplished using emulators that communicate from one application to another.) Banks relying on a single database may have stronger controls on data integrity than those with multiple databases and operating systems. However, it is rare to find a single automated system that handles data entry and all processing and control functions relevant to OTC and exchange-traded instruments. The systems used may be a combination of systems purchased from vendors, applications developed in-house, and legacy systems.

Incompatible systems can result in logistical obstacles because deal capture, data entry, and report generation will require multiple keying of data. Accordingly, controls and reconciliations that minimize the potential for corrupting data should be used when consolidating data obtained from multiple sources. If independent databases are used to support subsidiary systems, reconciliation controls should be in place at each point that data files come together. Regardless of how a bank combines automated systems and manual processes, management should ensure that appropriate validation processes ensure data integrity.

Periodic planning. Operations and support systems should receive periodic reviews to ensure that capacity, staffing, and the internal control environment support current and planned derivative activity. These reviews can be performed as a part of the annual budgeting and planning process, but should also be conducted as activity and plans change throughout the year.

Contingency planning. Plans should be in place to provide contingency systems and operations support in case of a natural disaster or systems failure. Contingency back-up plans should be comprehensive and include all critical support functions. The objective of the plan should be to restore business continuity as quickly and seamlessly as possible. Plans should be tested periodically. The overall contingency planning process should be reviewed and updated for market, product, and systems changes at least once a year.

Compliance Risk

Compliance risk is the risk to earnings or capital arising from violations, or nonconformance with, laws, rules, regulations, prescribed practices, or ethical standards. The risk also arises when the laws or rules governing certain bank products or activities of the bank's clients may be ambiguous or untested. Compliance risk exposes the institution to fines, civil money penalties, payment of damages, and the voiding of contracts. Compliance risk can lead to a diminished reputation, reduced franchise value, limited business opportunities, lessened expansion potential, and an inability to enforce contracts.

The legal authority of national banks to enter into derivative transactions is well-established. The OCC has recognized that national banks may enter into derivative transactions as *principal* when the bank may lawfully purchase and sell the underlying instrument or product for its own account, as a dealer or market-maker; or when the bank uses the transaction to hedge the risks arising from legally permissible activities.

A national bank may also enter into derivative transactions as principal or agent when the bank is acting as a financial intermediary for its customers and whether or not the bank has the legal authority to purchase or sell the underlying instrument for its own account. Accordingly, a national bank may enter into derivative transactions based on commodities or equity securities, even though the bank may not purchase (or may be restricted in purchasing) the underlying commodity or equity security for its own account.

Counterparty Authority

The enforceability of many OTC derivative contracts (e.g., swaps and options) in the event of counterparty insolvency has not been tested in the courts in all jurisdictions. Therefore, competent legal counsel should review applicable documents before such transactions are executed. Counsel should be familiar with the economic substance of the transaction, the laws of the jurisdictions in which the parties reside, and laws governing the market in which the instrument was traded. Whenever standardized documents are not used, contracts should be reviewed by counsel. Standard industry or trade association contracts should be reviewed whenever changes are made.

Limited End-Users

A requirement that bank counsel review all derivative contracts could entail significant legal expense and make derivative use uneconomical. An end-user (as well as dealers) can avoid much of this expense by using only standard industry contracts and addendums (e.g., the International Swaps and Derivatives Association, Inc., (ISDA) master agreement) and dealing only with counterparties domiciled in countries where there is high certainty of enforceability. Nonstandard clauses that are introduced in standardized contracts and addendums should be reviewed by legal counsel. With regard to counterparty authority and the legality and enforceability of the agreement, it may suffice for a limited end-user to obtain a legal opinion from its counterparty stating that the provisions of the agreement are enforceable and that it has the authority to enter into the transaction. If a limited end-user enters into a particularly novel transaction or does business with a high-risk counterparty (e.g., where legal uncertainty exists), then a more comprehensive legal review may be necessary.

Dealers and Active Position-Takers

National banks should make every effort to ensure that counterparties have the power and authority to enter into derivative transactions. The authority of a counterparty to engage in derivatives can be evidenced by corporate resolutions and certificates of incumbency. Additionally, banks should ensure that transactions are adequately documented. If adequate documentation of transactions is not obtained, enforcement of the transactions may be precluded under the relevant state law statute of frauds, which may require the existence of a written agreement for enforcement of a contract.

There are various methods by which a bank may reasonably satisfy itself that a counterparty has the legal capacity to engage in derivatives. For example, for governmental entities or for certain clients in regulated industries, a national bank should review relevant statutes or regulations delineating the powers of the entity. In other situations, a bank may need to examine the constitutive documents and other relevant materials of the counterparty; for example, for mutual fund clients, a bank should at least examine a fund's prospectus. In some cases, a bank may be able to achieve a level of reasonable satisfaction only upon the receipt and analysis of a well-reasoned opinion from competent counsel specifically addressing the issues of power and authority of the counterparty and the capacity of the individuals who will sign legal documents on behalf of the counterparty.

Some types of transactions may be more problematic than others. For example, a counterparty that has the power and authority to enter into interest rate swaps may not have the power or authority to engage in commodity derivative transactions. Also, the authority of certain fiduciaries to enter into derivative transactions may be limited by the governing instrument or by the Employee Retirement Income Security Act (ERISA). A national bank should ensure that all obligations arising from contemplated transactions with its counterparty are valid and enforceable. See also the discussion on transactions with undisclosed counterparties in the "Credit Risk" section.

Credit Enhancements

A bank should ensure that its rights with respect to any cash, securities, or other property pledged to the bank by a counterparty to margin, collateralize (secure), or guarantee a derivative contract are enforceable and exercisable and can be used upon the default of the counterparty to offset losses. To be reasonably sure that the pledged rights will be available if needed, the bank must have both access to, and the legal right to use the assets. For example, to establish reasonable access the counterparty should deliver pledged assets directly to the bank or to an independent escrow agent. Furthermore, bank counsel should give an opinion on whether the contract that governs the pledged assets is legally enforceable. See the "Credit Risk" and "Liquidity Risk" sections for more information on credit enhancements.

Bilateral Netting

As discussed above, a national bank must reasonably satisfy itself that the terms of any contract governing its derivative activities with a counterparty are legally sound. This is particularly important with respect to contract provisions that provide for the net settlement of balances between the bank and its counterparties.

Master settlement and close-out netting arrangements, to the extent *legally enforceable* (during the course of periodic payments and in the event of the insolvency of the counterparty), constitute a favorable means of reducing exposure to counterparty credit risk.

Settlement or payment netting involves netting payments between two counterparties, for the same date, the same currency, and under the same transaction or group of transactions, to a single payment.

Close-out (or default) netting arrangements involve netting the positive and negative current replacement values (mark-to-market) with respect to the non-defaulting party for each transaction under the agreement to a single sum, either positive or negative. If the sum of the netting is positive, then the defaulting counterparty owes that sum to the nondefaulting counterparty. If that amount is negative, the nondefaulting counterparty would pay that amount to the other party, provided no walkaway provisions exist.

Over the last few years, changes in the law have brought near certainty about the enforceability of bilateral close-out netting arrangements involving various derivative instruments during the insolvency proceedings of U.S. counterparties. The provisions of the Financial Institutions Reform, Recovery, and Enforcement Act of 1989 (FIRREA) provide that, in some instances, counterparties may net under master netting agreements consisting of swap agreements that are qualified financial contracts (as these terms are broadly defined) entered into with insured depository institutions placed in receivership or conservatorship. Subsequently, the 1990 amendments to the U.S. Bankruptcy Code extended to swap agreements (also broadly defined) immunity from (1) cherry-picking by a trustee in bankruptcy and (2) the automatic stay upon the filing of a petition in bankruptcy. Sections 401-407 of the Federal Deposit Insurance Corporation Improvement Act of 1991, the Payment Systems Risk Reduction Act (PSRRA), validated the netting of bilateral and multilateral payment obligations as contained in netting contracts entered into by financial institutions (as those terms are defined in the PSRRA).

The same degree of certainty does not apply to contracts with counterparties outside the United States. For national banks with significant exposures abroad, competent legal counsel should be consulted to more precisely quantify legal risk. **Where the legal enforceability of netting arrangements has not been established, national banks should not evaluate the risks of derivative transactions on a net basis.** In such instances, the benefits normally gained from such contracts will not be available. Thus, credit exposure may be grossly understated, and, therefore, improperly monitored. Only when the enforceability of close-out netting arrangements with foreign counterparties has a high degree of certainty, should national banks monitor their credit and liquidity risks for derivative transactions with such counterparties, on a net basis.

Multiproduct master agreements include all derivative transactions with a counterparty, regardless of the type of contract, in a single netting arrangement. National banks should recognize the potential legal risk in concentrating all derivative transactions with a counterparty under a multiproduct master agreement when applicable law does not clearly support the enforceability of the obligations arising out of such an agreement in the event of the default and insolvency of the bank's counterparty. In such cases, the close-out netting provisions may be unenforceable and the bank's exposure to counterparties may actually be the aggregate gross exposure on each outstanding derivative transaction.

When the enforceability of a multiproduct master agreement is uncertain but the enforceability of a single-product master is established, national banks should consider entering into single-product master netting agreements for different types of derivative transactions (e.g., currency options, commodity derivatives, and equity derivatives). In such cases, concentration risk is reduced and the bank will likely be able to rely on its net credit and liquidity exposure calculations under each agreement as an accurate assessment of its risk.

If a bank desires to avoid concentration risk and yet realize the potential benefits available from placing all derivative transactions with a counterparty under a single master agreement, it can enter into a master-master (or umbrella master) agreement, which will aggregate the net gains and losses across the individual single-product master netting agreements. If this agreement is deemed to be enforceable against a counterparty, then the bank will have realized the benefits of including all derivative transactions under a single-product master netting agreement. If it is not, the bank will have preserved the benefits that arise from entering into single-product master netting agreements.

The risk-based capital standards have recently been amended to recognize that bilateral netting agreements reduce credit risk. The 1994 amendment to 12 CFR 3 allows banks to bilaterally net contracts for risk-based capital purposes provided the bilateral netting agreement: 1) is in writing; 2) is not subject to a walkaway clause; and 3) creates a single legal obligation. Furthermore, the bank should: 1) obtain a written and reasoned legal opinion(s) stating with certainty that, in the event of a legal challenge, the court and the administrative authorities would find the bank's exposure to be the net amount; 2) establish and maintain procedures to monitor possible changes in the law and to ensure that bilateral netting contract continues to satisfy Part 3 requirements; and 3) maintain documentation in its files adequate to support netting under the contract. See the "Credit Risk" section for more information on bilateral netting.

Multilateral Netting

Multilateral netting is the netting of payments between a group of counterparties. Often, under a multilateral netting arrangement, a clearinghouse interposes itself as the legal counterparty. Exchange-traded futures and options clearinghouses are examples of multilateral netting arrangements. Clearinghouses for over-the-counter foreign exchange transactions operate in both the United States and the United Kingdom.

A national bank must ensure that any multilateral netting arrangement in which it participates does not increase its credit or systemic risks. When considering whether to enter into multilateral netting arrangements, national banks should ascertain: (a) the enforceability of the obligations of the participants, (b) the ability of the system to exercise freely and promptly the right of set-off with respect to any property deposited with the system by a defaulting participant as security for its obligations, (c) limitations on the obligations of nondefaulting participants to cover losses arising out of defaulted transactions, and (d) the financial integrity of the system as a whole. To this end, national banks should participate only in those multilateral netting facilities that meet the six minimum standards for netting and settlement schemes set forth in Part C of the Report of the Committee on Interbank Netting Schemes of the Central Banks of the Group of Ten Countries (also called the Lamfalussy Report) issued in November 1990 by the Bank of International Settlements. The six standards are summarized below.

- Netting schemes should have a well-founded legal basis under all relevant jurisdictions.

- Netting scheme participants should have a clear understanding of the impact of the particular scheme on each of the financial risks affected by the netting process.

- Multilateral netting schemes should have clearly defined procedures for the management of credit and liquidity risks that specify the respective responsibilities of the netting provider and the participants.

- Multilateral netting systems should, at a minimum, be capable of ensuring the timely completion of daily settlements in the event of an inability to settle by the participant with the largest single net debit position.

- Multilateral netting systems should have objective and publicly disclosed criteria for admission that permit fair and open access.

- All netting schemes should ensure the operational reliability of technical systems and the availability of back-up facilities capable of completing daily processing requirements.

Before entering into any multilateral netting arrangement (other than a clearinghouse associated with an established futures and options exchange), a national bank should consult with the OCC. Bank-specific approval will not be required. Generally, the OCC will review multilateral clearinghouses case by case. If the OCC is satisfied that the clearinghouse will meet the Lamfalussy standards, a universal approval for national bank membership will be granted. National banks considering membership in a multilateral clearinghouse should ask the OCC whether it approves of national banks joining that particular clearinghouse. See the "Credit Risk" section for more information on multilateral netting.

Physical Commodities

National banks may engage in physical commodity transactions in order to manage the risks arising out of commodity derivative transactions if they meet the following conditions:

- Any physical transactions supplement the bank's existing risk management activities, constitute a nominal percentage of the bank's risk management activities, are used only to manage risk arising from otherwise permissible (customer-driven) banking activities, and are not entered into for speculative purposes; and

- Before entering into any such physical transactions, the bank has submitted a detailed plan for the activity to the OCC and the plan has been approved.

The OCC has concluded that a national bank may engage in physical commodity transactions in order to manage the risks of physical commodity financial derivative transactions. However, to ensure that the bank understands the risks of physical hedging activities, management must first develop a detailed plan, which should be approved by the bank's board and the supervisory staff of the OCC before the bank engages in such activities.

Upon OCC approval, a national bank may engage in the activities only under the conditions specified above, and any other conditions that may be imposed on the bank by the OCC's supervisory staff. All activities must be conducted in accordance with safe and sound banking principles.

Financial derivative transactions with respect to bank-eligible precious metals (gold, silver, platinum, palladium, and copper) are not subject to this guideline.

Equity Derivatives

The OCC has permitted a national bank to make interest payments on customer deposit accounts based on the percentage increase, if any, in the S&P Index from the date the account is opened until maturity, and to hedge its interest obligations to the holders of deposit accounts with futures contracts in the S&P Index. In finding these transactions permissible for national banks, the OCC concluded that offering the account is within the expressly authorized power of national banks to receive deposits. The OCC further concluded that a national bank's purchase and sale of S&P Index futures to hedge its interest obligations on the deposit was incidental to the bank's expressly authorized deposit-taking authority. In reaching these conclusions, the OCC recognized that because the futures would be cash settled, the bank would not acquire any ownership interest in the securities comprising the S&P Index.[1]

National banks may enter into matched and unmatched equity and equity index swaps (equity derivative swaps) as agent or principal. A national bank may hedge risks arising from any unmatched equity derivative swaps by purchasing and selling exchange-traded futures and options, government securities, or forward contracts. Moreover, banks warehousing equity derivative swaps may use futures contracts, options, and similar over-the-counter instruments that are settled in cash to hedge the aggregate unmatched positions in the portfolio. In finding equity derivative swap activities permissible for national banks, the OCC recognized that a bank engaging in matched and unmatched equity derivative swaps acts as a financial intermediary, just as it does in its deposit and lending

---

[1]Sentence revised October 2001.

activities. All these activities involve making and receiving payments on behalf of customers.

Capital Issues

The board of directors and senior management should ensure that the bank maintains sufficient capital to support the risks that may arise from its derivative activities. Significant changes in the size or scope of a bank's activities should prompt an analysis of the adequacy of the amount of capital supporting those activities. This analysis, which may be incorporated into the bank's periodic review of capital adequacy for all activities, should be approved by the board or senior management and be available for bank examiner review. Senior management should ensure that the bank meets all regulatory capital standards for financial derivative activities.

Under risk-based capital requirements, national banks must hold capital for counterparty credit risks in financial derivative contracts. These requirements are specified in 12 CFR 3, appendix A. Appendix A also specifies that the OCC will pay particular attention to any bank with significant exposure to declines in the economic value of its capital due to changes in interest rates. The OCC may require such a bank to hold additional capital.

In August 1996, the OCC amended the risk-based capital standards to incorporate a measure for market risk. For purposes of that regulation, market risk means exposure to losses from movements in market prices in a bank's trading account, foreign exchange positions, and commodity positions. Under appendix B, any bank with significant market risk must measure that risk using its own internal value-at-risk model, subject to the parameters in the appendix, and hold commensurate capital.

As these and any other modifications or additions to capital requirements are adopted, bank management must ensure that all financial derivative activities are properly incorporated into the bank's minimum capital levels.

Accounting Issues

Accounting guidance for financial derivative instruments is not comprehensive. Financial Accounting Standard (FAS) 52 and FAS 80 address only futures transactions. Regulatory accounting principles (RAP), set forth in the *Instructions to Consolidated Reports of*

Condition and Income, address only futures, forwards, and options. The lack of comprehensive GAAP or RAP guidance for derivatives has led to inconsistent accounting treatment for some products, particularly swaps.

Both the Financial Accounting Standards Board (FASB) and the OCC are studying accounting standards for derivative transactions. The OCC is working to develop a consistent regulatory accounting policy for all derivative products. In cooperation with other U.S. banking agencies, the OCC will consider the impact of accounting rules on business decisions, with a view to minimizing regulatory burden. As part of this initiative, the Federal Financial Institutions Examination Council (FFIEC) has announced plans to bring call reports in conformity with GAAP. This change will become effective for reports filed as of March 31, 1997.

Until more authoritative guidance on derivatives is issued, each bank should review its accounting practices and documentation to ensure consistency with the strategies and objectives approved by its board.

Risk Management of Financial Derivatives

Tier I and Tier II Dealers Request Letter

Below is a comprehensive list of suggested request items for Tier I and Tier II dealers. Because the activities of bank derivative dealers vary widely, examiners should tailor the request letter to the specific activities and risks faced by the bank and the specific area targeted for examination.

Before requesting information from the bank, examiners should discuss their examination scope with examiners working in other areas of the bank who may have requested similar information. This will help avoid duplicative requests for information and reduce the burden on the bank of compiling the material.

Senior Management and Board Oversight

____ 1. Board minutes and relevant committee minutes (e.g., asset liability management committee (ALCO), audit, new products), including handouts and presentation materials, since the last examination.

____ 2. Written policies and procedures, including limits, for relevant areas such as treasury, trading, new products, risk control, audit, credit, funding, operations, accounting, code of ethics, legal and compliance.

____ 3. Organizational charts for key functional areas (e.g., treasury, trading, risk control, credit, funding, operations, audit and compliance).

____ 4. Brief biographies or resumes of managers of units responsible for derivative activities.

____ 5. Job descriptions for key positions responsible for derivative activities, including officer responsibilities and authority levels.

____ 6. Compensation plan for key line managers, traders, and salespeople.

____ 7. Internal and external audit, risk control, and compliance and consultant reports (including management responses) since the last examination.

____ 8.   Business and strategic plans for relevant areas.

____ 9.   Monthly budget variance reports for the year-to-date on a consolidated basis and for all relevant profit centers.

____ 10.   Revenue and earnings reports for the prior year and year-to-date by month on a consolidated basis and for all relevant profit centers.

____ 11.   Consolidated risk management reports for targeted activities .

____ 12.   Summary of monthly derivatives volume (by notional and transactional amounts) for the prior year and year-to-date.

____ 13.   Summary of the customer base (e.g., retail in proportion to institutional).

____ 14.   Samples of derivatives marketing presentations, advertisements, and other sales documents.

Price Risk

____ 15.   Price risk monitoring reports used by senior management and line managers (including limit monitoring).

____ 16.   Access to price risk limit exception reports for the desired sample period, including subsequent approvals.

____ 17.   Access to derivatives portfolio position reports for the desired sample period.

____ 18.   Description of the method used to measure price risk including source, key assumptions such as historical observation periods, confidence levels, correlations, database parameters, and updates.

____ 19.   Results of portfolio stress testing.

___ 20.   Price risk model validation reports and management's responses, if applicable.

___ 21.   If available, breakdown of sources of trading/positioning profits for relevant profit centers (e.g., customer trading income, dealer spread, positioning income, proprietary trading income, net interest income).

Liquidity Risk

___ 22.   Access to derivatives portfolio cash flow reports for the desired sample period.

___ 23.   Liquidity risk monitoring reports used by senior management and line management.

___ 24.   Contingency funding plan.

Foreign Exchange Risk

___ 25.   Description of the methods used to identify, measure, monitor, and control capital exposure from foreign currency translation.

___ 26.   Management reports detailing all exposures from foreign currency translation.

___ 27.   Reports detailing hedge efficiency and performance related to capital exposure from foreign currency translation.

Credit Risk

___ 28.   Access to a list of transactions with collateral enhancements, margining agreements, third-party guarantees, or early termination clauses (both one-way and two-way).

___ 29.   Description of the method used to measure presettlement and settlement credit risk exposure including source, key assumptions such as historical observation periods, confidence levels, correlations, database parameters and updates.

___ 30.   Credit risk model validation reports and management's responses, if applicable.

___ 31.   Credit risk monitoring reports used by senior and line management (including limit monitoring).

___ 32.   Access to a list of counterparty credit lines and credit line availability. If available, reports broken out by dealer and end-user/customer and internal risk rating.

___ 33.   Counterparty credit risk rating report that aggregates bank-wide credit exposure by counterparty, including that originating from commercial lending relationships.

___ 34.   Counterparty credit concentration reports sorted by external factors (e.g., countries, regions, industries), internal factors (e.g., exposure, tenors, risk ratings), and type of counterparty (e.g., interbank, corporate), if possible.

___ 35.   Large deal reports for the desired sample period.

___ 36.   Credit policy and limit exception reports (e.g., counterparty credit limit exceptions, past due counterparty reviews, and documentation exceptions) including subsequent approvals.

___ 37.   Past-due, nonperforming, or deteriorating trend counterparty credit line reports.

___ 38.   List of customer transactions terminated or amended during the prior 12 months (or shorter period if deemed appropriate) with reason for action.

Transaction Risk

___ 39.   Flow charts of processing and reporting flows.

___ 40.   Information used to evaluate back office operational efficiency (e.g., average hours, overtime, number of transactions processed per employee, volume/ratio of disputed, unconfirmed, or failed trades) and incurred penalties.

___ 41. Description of front and back office systems configuration (hardware and software), including spreadsheet systems.

___ 42. Operational exceptions reports (aging, failed trades, off-market trades, outstanding items, suspense items, miscellaneous losses, etc.).

___ 43. Summary of most recent account reconcilements between front and back office and general ledger and subsidiary ledgers or a description of the process.

___ 44. Brokerage commission and fee reports.

___ 45. Description of derivatives valuation process (who, how, frequency, etc.).

___ 46. Details of valuation reserve accounts including current balance, reserve methodology, and accounting treatment.

___ 47. Systems disaster recovery plan.

Compliance Risk

___ 48. Pending litigation or customer complaints lodged against the bank relating to derivative activities.

___ 49. Legal documentation exception reports.

___ 50. Access to compliance program procedures and supporting workpapers for recent reports.

Risk Management Active Position-Takers/Limited End-Users
of Financial Derivatives Request Letter

Below is a comprehensive list of suggested request items for active position-takers and limited end-users. Because the activities of active position-takers and limited end-users vary widely, examiners should tailor the request letter to the specific activities of the bank and the specific area targeted for examination.

Before requesting information from the bank, examiners should discuss their examination scope with examiners working in other areas of the bank who may have requested similar information. This will help avoid duplicative requests for information and reduce the burden on the bank of compiling the material.

Senior Management and Board Oversight

____ 1. Board minutes and relevant committee minutes (e.g., ALCO, audit, new products) including handouts and presentation materials since the last examination.

____ 2. Written policies and procedures, including limits, for relevant areas such as treasury, new products, credit, liquidity, operations, accounting, risk control, audit, code of ethics, legal and compliance.

____ 3. Organizational charts for key functional areas (e.g., treasury, credit, liquidity, operations, risk control, audit, legal and compliance).

____ 4. Internal and external audit, risk control, and compliance and consultant reports and management responses since the last examination.

____ 5. Business and strategic plans.

____ 6. Budget and variance reports year-to-date.

____ 7. Revenue and earnings reports for the prior year and year-to-date.

____ 8.   Consolidated risk management reports (interest rate, credit, and liquidity risks).

____ 9.   Summary of derivative transactions for the desired sample period (by notional and transactional amounts).

____ 10.   Risk management or hedging reports showing effectiveness of strategies.

Interest Rate Risk

____ 11.   Interest rate risk management reports used by senior management and line managers (including limit monitoring).

____ 12.   Access to a description of the method used to measure interest rate risk and access to supporting documents describing key parameters and assumptions such as interest rate scenarios, prepayments, maturity and repricing characteristics of indeterminate maturity accounts, and new business.

____ 13.   Results of interest rate stress test reports.

____ 14.   Results of back-testing of interest rate risk methodology (for accrual earnings-at-risk).

____ 15.   Interest rate risk model validation reports and management responses (as applicable).

Liquidity Risk

___ 16. Liquidity risk monitoring reports used by senior management and line management.

___ 17. Contingency funding plan.

Credit Risk

___ 18. Access to a list of transactions with collateral enhancements, margining agreements, third-party guarantees, or early termination clauses (both one-way and two-way).

___ 19. Description of the method used to measure credit risk.

___ 20. Credit risk model validation reports and management's responses, if applicable.

___ 21. Credit risk reports used by senior management and line management (including limit monitoring).

___ 22. Credit policy and limit exception reports.

Transaction Risk

___ 23. Flow charts of processing and reporting flows.

___ 24. Information used to evaluate back office operational efficiency (e.g., average hours, overtime, number of transactions processed per employee, volume/ratio of disputed, unconfirmed, or failed trades) and any incurred penalties.

___ 25. Description of front and back office systems configuration (hardware and software), including spreadsheet systems.

___ 26.   Summary of most recent account reconcilements between front and back office and general ledger and subsidiary ledgers or process description.

___ 27.   Operational exceptions reports (e.g., aging, failed trades, outstanding items, suspense items, miscellaneous losses).

___ 28.   Description of derivative valuation process (who, how, frequency, etc.).

Compliance Risk

___ 29.   Pending litigation related to derivative activities.

___ 30.   Legal documentation exception reports.

___ 31.   Access to compliance program procedures and supporting workpapers for recent reports.

Risk Management of Financial Derivatives

Examination Procedures

General Procedures

The following procedures should be used when examining the derivatives activities of national banks and nationally chartered federal agencies and branches. The procedures in the first section will help the examiner determine the nature of the bank's use of derivatives. After that determination has been made, the examiner should proceed to the appropriate section (i.e., Tier I and Tier II dealers or active position-takers and limited end-users). When examining limited end-users whose only derivatives exposure is in the form of structured notes, follow the specific procedures for structured notes in that section.

Objective: To evaluate the bank's participation in derivatives markets and set the examination scope.

1.   Review OCC documents to identify any previous issues with derivatives that require follow-up.

   ☐ Prior examination reports.
   ☐ Overall summary comments.
   ☐ Work papers from prior examinations.
   ☐ OCC approvals, if applicable.

2.   Prepare and submit a request letter to management.

3.   Review request information for significant changes in derivatives activities since the prior examination. Consider the following:

- Management.
- Products and activities.
- Philosophy and strategy.
- Risk profile.
- Policies and procedures.
- Staffing.
- Front, middle and back office operations and systems.

4. Discuss with management the bank's strategies, objectives, and plans regarding derivatives.

5. Determine key personnel involved in derivatives activities and their reporting lines.

6. If dealing is conducted, determine the nature of the bank's dealing activities and if the bank is a Tier I or Tier II dealer. Consider the following:

- The types and complexity of derivatives instruments offered.
- Whether the bank actively or selectively makes market quotes.
- Whether the bank develops its own products.
- Whether the bank actively solicits business with a dedicated sales force.
- The customer base – retail, corporate, financial institutions, other market-makers/professionals.
- The existence of proprietary trading activities.
- Customer transaction flow in proportion to dealer transaction flow.
- The size and extent of open positions relative to matched transactions.
- Transaction volume.
- Risk profile and trends in value-at-risk (VAR), particularly relative to corporate capital and earnings.

7. For banks that are end-users of derivatives, determine the nature of active position-taking and limited end-user activity.

Consider the following:

- The level of derivatives transaction volume relative to the size of the bank.
- The types and complexity of derivatives instruments used.
- Whether instruments are used to actively manage interest rate risk exposure or as investment substitutes.

8. Obtain an overview of performance by derivatives portfolio used in trading (e.g., P&L) or risk management activity (e.g., yield enhancement or hedge effectiveness). Ascertain the significance of derivatives revenue. Consider the following:

- Profits/losses from accrual books and mark-to-market books.
- Earnings composition and trends.

Based on the above procedures, determine the nature of the bank's derivatives activities and select the appropriate procedures to use in examining those activities.

Tier I and Tier II Dealers

Quantity of Risk

Conclusion: The quantity of risk is (low, moderate, high).

Objective: To determine the nature of the bank's trading activities.

1.   Review and discuss the nature of the bank's trading activities (including recent trends) with senior management, salespeople, and traders. Determine:

- Overall risk positioning philosophy and hedging strategy.
- Types of instruments and markets traded, including new products.
- Product concentrations.
- Complexity of instruments traded (i.e., plain vanilla vs. exotic).
- Key contributors to earnings.
- Various functional trading desks (e.g., FX, interest rate, commodity, equity instruments).
- Daily average number of trades, the dollar volume, and trends.
- Average and maximum maturity of forward trading.
- Primary geographic trading centers, including centralized risk trading centers.
- Communication/strategies across geographic trading centers.
- Markets in which the bank acts as a market-maker.
- Other market niches.
- Percentage of corporate/interbank/proprietary trading.
- Nature and volume of intrabank and intra-affiliate trading.

Objective: To determine the quantity of price risk resulting from derivatives activities.

1.   Evaluate the relative contribution of sources of trading revenue such as:

- Retail spread or customer mark-up.
- Dealer (interbank) spread.
- Positioning.
- Proprietary trading.
- Arbitrage.
- Particular products.

2. Review the volatility of trading revenue over time. This review should usually be conducted for each portfolio. Review monthly, weekly, and year-to-date trends over the past 9 to 12 months and obtain any written explanation of earnings performance. Over time, compare:

- The reasonableness of trading revenue against price risk exposure (value-at-risk).
- The level of actual price risk exposure against price risk limits.
- The usage of the limits and number and type of limit excesses.
- Trading revenue against budgeted results.
- Trading revenue in comparison to peer and/or in light of market conditions.

3. Determine whether there were any external market disruptions since the last examination affecting the bank's trading activities. If so, determine the bank's response.

4. Obtain daily risk exposure reports for the desired sample period. Select time periods that evidence unusual earnings results or significant price volatility. Evaluate trends in risk positions over time. Discuss the level of intraday positions with trading management. This analysis may be conducted both on a consolidated basis and by product, currency, or portfolio. In light of current strategies, risk limits, dealer qualifications, market conditions, and earnings, evaluate:

- Overnight and intraday open risk positions and compare against limits.
- Limits usage, as well as the volume and causes of limit excesses.
- Size of individual positions.

5. Review the structure of trading limits, including informal trading desk/room limits, in view of trading activities. Evaluate whether limits:

- Are consistent with articulated strategy.
- Are reasonable in light of trader qualifications and recent profit/loss experience.
- Adequately control exposures to identified price risk in normal and distressed market conditions.
- Adequately reflect the liquidity differences between markets and instruments under normal and stressed conditions.
- Are allocated among dealing desks in a reasonable and controlled manner.
- Are not set so high that risk-taking is allowed to reach unreasonable levels or that meaningful shifts in risk-taking go undetected.
- Are reassessed on an ongoing basis and that appropriate revisions are made to reflect changes in strategies, staff, or market dynamics.
- Are communicated in a timely manner to appropriate parties within the bank (e.g., traders, risk managers, and operations).

6. Determine that price risk limits and price risk exposures are derived consistently and are therefore comparable to each other.

Objective: To determine the quantity of liquidity risk resulting from derivatives activities.

1. Obtain daily maturity and cash flow gap reports from the trading desk for the desired sample period. In particular,

review gaps during time periods that show unusual profits/losses or periods of significant price risk volatility. Evaluate the size of the gaps relative to the risks present, current strategies, risk limits, and trader expertise.

2. Evaluate the bank's use of credit enhancements, margin arrangements, and third-party guarantees and their impact on the level of liquidity risk. Determine that these arrangements are not being used to take inappropriate risk positions.

3. Evaluate the bank's the use of early termination triggers and their impact on the level of liquidity risk.

Objective: To determine the quantity of foreign currency translation risk resulting from derivatives activities.

1. Evaluate the level of earnings and capital exposed to changes in foreign currency rates. Determine if:

   - All relevant exposures are captured and reported.
   - The level of risk is appropriate for the institution.
   - Trends or fluctuations in risk are identified, reported, and consistent with articulated strategy. Identify instances where management decides to leave exposure unhedged and determine whether actions are reasonable.

2. Evaluate the effectiveness of foreign currency translation risk hedging activities. Consider the following:

   - Whether assumptions are appropriate.
   - Instances where hedging is done in other than the indigenous currency or interest rate. In particular, consider the bank's tactics regarding currencies that are tied to another currency or to a basket of currencies.
   - Hedge performance under stressed scenarios.
   - Frequency of hedge adjustments.

3.   Review and discuss future plans and strategies with management regarding anticipated changes in foreign currency translation exposure.

Objective: To determine the quantity of credit risk resulting from derivatives activities.

1.   Review credit risk monitoring reports used by management. Determine sources of credit risk and evaluate trends. Consider the following:

- Counterparty downgrades or deterioration.
- Past due counterparty payments.
- Counterparty concentrations.
- Undisclosed counterparties.
- Settlement risk exposure.

2.   Evaluate the adequacy of the process for underwriting counterparties. Select a sample of counterparties from the list of derivatives counterparties broken out by dealer and end-user/customer. Review credit files for the sample counterparties. Determine if:

- Files are current and contain sufficient information to document an informed credit decision, including purpose, source of repayment, and collateral.
- Credit evaluations aggregate limits for derivatives with the limits established for other activities, including commercial lending.
- Distinct limits are established for settlement and presettlement risk and are well supported.
- Risk ratings are accurate and supported.
- Management assessment of creditworthiness incorporates the impact of the counterparty's use of derivatives contracts on its financial condition.

Objective: To determine the quantity of transaction risk resulting from derivatives activities.

1. Evaluate the efficiency of the operating environment. To gain an understanding of where transaction risk may exist, follow an actual trade ticket through the processing system, from trader's verbal commitment to final booking. Evaluate:

   - The length of time from a dealer's verbal commitment to the deal's entry into the accounting system.
   - Whether the back office has a queuing mechanism to ensure that all transactions are processed in a timely manner.
   - Workloads of operations personnel. Evaluate average hours worked per week, overtime pay, and number of transactions processed per employee.
     - Compare the bank's information to that of a peer bank, if available.
     - If applicable, review for significant adverse trends in losses during times of long hours for trade processing personnel.
   - The capacity and ability of the systems and staff to handle present and projected future volumes and types of transactions.

2. Review operations exception reports (aging, failed trades, off-market trades, outstanding items, suspense items, miscellaneous losses). Evaluate the level and nature of exceptions. Determine whether appropriate approval for exceptions was obtained when warranted.

3. Discuss with operations management any unconfirmed or disputed trades that have occurred over the past 12 months. Evaluate the source and nature of the discrepancies and disputes and their ultimate resolution. Review the adequacy of documentation.

4. Evaluate the effectiveness of the credit operations department. Determine if:

- The bank has sufficient capacity to run all transactions through the credit exposure model at reasonable intervals.
- Credit exposure calculations are performed or verified by people independent of the trading function.
- Credit lines (including lines for presettlement, settlement, and tenor) and usage are updated and changed on the system in a timely manner.

5. Review current systems capabilities and planned upgrades or enhancements. Determine that:

- Front office risk management requirements are properly considered.
- Systems planning and implementation schedules are consistent with transaction growth and the current and planned level of business activity.
- Access controls are adequate.

Objective: To determine the quantity of compliance risk resulting from derivatives activities.

1. Review legal documentation exception reports. Evaluate the source, nature, and level of exceptions.

2. Discuss with management pending litigation or customer complaints lodged against the bank relating to derivatives activities. Evaluate the source, nature, and level of customer litigation/complaints.

3. Verify that the bank has reported its derivatives transactions consistent with call report instructions.

Objective: To determine the quantity of reputation risk resulting from derivatives activities.

1.   From discussions with management and traders, determine the credit rating and market acceptance of the bank as a counterparty in the markets. If the bank recently experienced a ratings downgrade, ascertain the impact of the credit rating downgrade on their ability to manage risk. Banks may find counterparties less willing to deal with them (e.g., counterparties report they are full up or decline long-dated transactions, calls for collateral, or early termination).

Objective: To determine the quantity of strategic risk resulting from derivatives activities.

1.   Review and discuss future plans and strategies with management. Consider the following:

- Marketing/trading strategies.
- New product or business initiatives.
- New system or model upgrades.
- Anticipated changes in the risk profile

Tier I and Tier II Dealers

Quality of Risk Management

Conclusion: The quality of risk management is (strong, satisfactory, weak).

Policy

Conclusion: The board (has, has not) established effective policies relating to the bank's derivatives activities.

Objective: To evaluate the adequacy of derivatives policies relating to price risk.

1. Evaluate the adequacy of price risk management policies and procedures. Determine if they:

   - Establish price risk limits.
   - Require periodic review of price risk exposure.
   - Describe the method used to calculate price risk exposure.
   - Describe the acceptable process for market valuation.
   - Require independent validation of price risk models.
   - Require periodic stress testing.
   - Require periodic back-testing of price risk models.
   - Address reporting and control of off-market trades, if permitted.
   - Require annual board approval.
   - Require preparation and distribution of position reports by an independent party, without intervention by the trader or risk-taking unit.
   - Require timely notification of actual or probable limit exceptions.
   - Require prompt consideration of all limit exception requests (generally, approvals should be obtained from the next higher level of management).
   - Address monitoring and tracking of limit breaks and exception approvals.

2. Determine whether management's policy for review and updating of assumptions underlying the pricing, revaluation, and risk measurement models is reasonable. Determine whether management complies with the policy.

Objective: To evaluate the adequacy of derivatives policies relating to liquidity risk.

1. Evaluate the adequacy of liquidity risk management policies and procedures. Determine if they:

    - Require the incorporation, if material, of derivatives and corresponding collateral, margin arrangements, and early termination agreements into liquidity-related management information systems and contingency plans.
    - Detail circumstances in which the bank will honor noncontractual early termination requests.
    - Describe when the bank will provide credit enhancements.
    - Limit the amount of assets that can be encumbered by collateral and margin arrangements (such limits are generally determined after performing analyses to identify requirements under adverse scenarios).
    - Limit the amount of collateral tied to common triggers (e.g., credit rating).
    - Require annual board approval.

2. Determine whether established limits adequately control the range of liquidity risks. Determine that the limits are appropriate for the level of activity.

3. Evaluate the bank's policies addressing the use of early termination triggers. Determine if they:

    - Discourage use of early termination triggers where the bank is subject to termination.

- Allow early termination triggers only after careful consideration of the impact on price risk exposure and bank liquidity.
- Clearly define the circumstances under which management will honor a request for early termination when it is not part of the customer's contract.

Objective: To evaluate the adequacy of derivatives policies relating to foreign currency translation risk.

1. Evaluate the adequacy of foreign currency translation risk management policies and procedures for derivatives activities. Determine if they:

   - Discuss the objectives of the program to manage the level of capital exposed to foreign currency revaluations. Ensure these objectives are clearly articulated, measurable, and reasonable.
   - Discuss issues regarding activities in countries possessing illiquid or nondeliverable currencies.
   - Define exposure limits within which the bank seeks to operate.
   - Discuss both branches and affiliates.
   - Clearly identify the persons responsible for managing the level of capital exposed to foreign currency revaluations, and require that they be independent of other trading areas.
   - Define whether exposure will be managed on a centralized or decentralized basis.
   - Define requirements for limit exceptions and approvals.
   - List appropriate products to be used to hedge exposure, and identify individuals responsible for monitoring hedge performance.
   - Provide prudent safeguards against adverse currency fluctuations.
   - Require annual approval by the board or appropriate committee.

Objective: To evaluate the adequacy of derivatives policies relating to credit risk.

1. Evaluate the adequacy of credit risk management policies and procedures. Determine if they:

    - Establish guidelines for derivatives portfolio credit quality, concentrations, and tenors.
    - Require at least annual counterparty review and assignment of risk ratings.
    - Establish and define formal reporting requirements on counterparty credit exposure.
    - Require designation of separate counterparty limits for presettlement and settlement credit risk.
    - Require independent monitoring and reporting of aggregate credit exposure for each counterparty (including all credit exposure from other business lines) and comparison with limits.
    - Describe the mechanism for policy and limit exception approvals and reporting, including situations where a counterparty credit line is exceeded because of a large market move (e.g., collateral calls, up-front payments, termination).
    - Require an evaluation of the appropriateness of customer transactions.
    - Address transactions with undisclosed counterparties.
    - Address permissibility and reporting of off-market trades (including historical rate roll-overs).
    - Address administration of nonperforming contracts. (This policy should be consistent with policies adopted in traditional lending divisions.)
    - Address allowance allocations and require derivatives credit reserves to cover expected losses.
    - Require annual board approval.

2. Evaluate the bank's policies and written agreements regarding

the use of credit enhancements. Determine if they:

- Require evaluating the counterparty's ability to provide and meet collateral or margin requirements at inception and during the term of the agreement.
- Address acceptable types of instruments for collateral and margining.
- Address the ability to substitute assets.
- Address time of posting (i.e., at inception, upon change in risk rating, upon change in level of exposure).
- Establish valuation methods (i.e., sources of pricing, timing of revaluation).
- Address the ability to hypothecate contracts.
- Address physical control over assets.
- Address dispute resolution.

3. Evaluate bank policies covering customer appropriateness. Determine if they:

- Clearly outline specific responsibilities for both credit and marketing officers.
- Clearly define the type of documentation, if any, to be maintained by both credit and marketing personnel.
- Define the types of disclosures or representations, if any, to be made to customers.
- Provide guidance to marketers on avoiding the implication of an advisory relationship.
- Provide a framework for evaluating counterparty sophistication and transaction complexity.
- Require an independent party periodically review counterparty exposures to identify new and significant mark-to-market exposures.
- Require that significant adverse exposures are brought to senior management's attention.

4. Determine whether the bank trades with investment advisors or other third parties acting as agents on behalf of undisclosed counterparties. Determine if:

- The bank has developed a credit policy that addresses trades involving undisclosed counterparties.
- The credit policy limits exposure to undisclosed counterparties and provides for periodic monitoring. Types of limits and controls could include:
  - Requiring careful review and approval of the practice by senior management and the board.
  - Restricting transactions to agents and other intermediaries to only those persons and firms known to be reputable and who agree to the bank's risk management requirements.
  - Restricting transactions to an approved list of counterparties.
  - Limiting the size of transactions with undisclosed counterparties individually and in aggregate.
  - Limiting transactions to very liquid, spot FX or short-term forward transactions involving high-quality securities with regular DVP settlement.
  - Requiring third-party guarantees or collateral to ensure performance.
- The bank has obtained legal opinions regarding the enforceability of any written agreements.
- The bank has ensured compliance with the "know your customer" requirement of applicable money laundering regulations.

Objective: To evaluate the adequacy of derivatives policies relating to transaction risk.

1. Evaluate the adequacy of transaction risk management policies and procedures for derivatives activities. Determine if they address:

    - Segregation of duties between trading, processing, and payment functions.

- Description of accounts.
- Trade entry and transaction documentation.
- Confirmations.
- Settlement.
- Exception reporting.
- Documentation tracking and reporting.
- Revaluation.
- Reconciliations including frequency.
- Discrepancies and disputed trades.
- Broker accounts.
- Accounting treatment.
- Management reporting.

2. Determine whether personnel policies require that key employees take two weeks of consecutive vacation.

Objective: To evaluate the adequacy of derivatives policies relating to compliance risk.

1. Determine that policies require appropriate legal review of all relevant activities including new products, counterparty or agreement forms, and netting arrangements.

2. Obtain a copy of the bank's accounting procedures and review for conformance with the relevant sections regarding trading and hedging transactions within authoritative pronouncements by the Financial Accounting Standards Board and call report instructions.

3. In the absence of authoritative accounting guidance, determine whether the bank's accounting policy for derivatives transactions is reasonable and consistently applied.

Objective: To evaluate the adequacy of derivatives policies relating to reputation risk.

1. Determine if the board established a code of ethics/conflict of interest policy for trading activities that provides an adequate

framework to control risk to the bank's reputation. Determine if the policy:

- Prohibits any deceptive, dishonest, or unfair practice.
- Provides for a mechanism to monitor gifts and gratuities.
- Prohibits false or materially misleading marketing material.
- Provides for the disclosures and consents necessary to avoid conflicts of interest.
- Provides for a system to determine the existence of possible control relationships.
- Prohibits the use of confidential, nonpublic information without the written approval of affected counterparties.
- Prohibits the improper use of funds held on another's behalf.
- Designates specific principals to supervise personnel and business conduct in general.
- Adopts price mark-up guidelines.
- Allocates responsibility for transactions with the bank's own employees and employees of other dealers.

2. If the bank uses derivatives in a fiduciary capacity, contact the examiners reviewing "Fiduciary Activities" for their assessment of how derivatives are managed in a fiduciary capacity and the adequacy of related policies and procedures.

Objective: To evaluate the adequacy of derivatives policies relating to strategic risk.

1. Determine if the board has established a new product policy. Determine that the policy requires that all relevant areas, such as the business line, systems, risk control, credit, accounting, legal, operations, tax, and regulatory compliance, evaluate risks and controls. Determine if the policy:

- Defines a new product or activity.

- Establishes a process to identify new product transactions. Determine if new product documentation is required to:
  - Describe the product.
  - Explain the product's consistency with business strategies and objectives.
  - Identify and evaluate risks and describe how they will be managed.
  - Describe the limit and exception approval processes.
  - Describe capital allocations.
  - Describe accounting procedures.
  - Summarize operational procedures and controls.
  - Detail approval of legal documentation.
  - Address other legal and regulatory issues.
  - Explain tax implications.
  - Describe the ongoing maintenance process.

Processes

Conclusion: Management and the board (have, have not) implemented effective processes to manage derivatives activities.

Objective: To determine the adequacy of processes relating to management of price risk in derivatives activities.

1. Evaluate the manner in which trading strategies are formulated, executed, and monitored. Consider the following:

    - Line management's day-to-day oversight of trading activities.
    - The limits and restrictions on delegated authorities.
    - Requirements for approving trading in new products, markets, and extended maturities.
    - Management's authority and willingness to modify or override trader decisions (using offsetting positions or specific instructions).
    - Modifications in varying market conditions.

2. Obtain a list of recent price risk limit exceptions. Determine

whether the exceptions were identified and approved on a timely basis. Determine whether the basis and timeliness of approval were reasonable and within the approver's authority. Evaluate the level and nature of the exceptions.

3. Determine that the types of pricing models used and their capacities are appropriate for the nature and volume of business conducted. Determine the person(s) responsible for developing and maintaining the models.

4. Evaluate the method used to measure price risk exposure. Determine who developed and maintains the system. Assess whether the method is commensurate with the nature and complexity of the activity conducted. Determine whether:

   - Price risk is measured on a desk, country, regional, and global basis.
   - The bank's systems can aggregate price risk exposure across all products, desks, branches, and globally.
   - The method considers the characteristics of the underlying instruments in view of the following:
     - Tenor of the instrument.
     - Changes in price under varying market conditions, in response to changes in liquidity, etc.
     - Estimated holding period or time to close or hedge the position.
   - The methodology expresses risk as a percentage of current earnings or capital.
   - The exposure arising from a change in applicable major market factors, such as interest rates, foreign exchange rates or market volatility, can be aggregated, evaluated, and reported in a timely manner.
   - The system facilitates stress testing.

5. If the price risk measurement system does not include all sources of price risk exposure, estimate the percentage of risk

captured by the system. Determine whether senior management is aware of coverage levels and if the omissions are reasonable in view of the circumstances.

6. Determine whether management performs adequate stress testing. Evaluate:

    - The basis for stress scenarios.
    - The reasonableness of stress scenarios.
    - Whether the frequency of stress testing is appropriate.
    - Whether stress tests incorporate the interconnectedness of risks.
    - Whether senior management and the board are apprised of the results of portfolio stress testing.

Objective: To determine the adequacy of processes relating to management of liquidity risk in derivatives activities.

1. Determine whether the bank maintains closeout cost reserves. If so, determine whether the method for calculating the reserve is reasonable.

2. Determine that the bank's liquidity risk management function has a separate reporting line from traders and marketers.

3. Ascertain whether good communication exists between derivatives managers and persons responsible for domestic and foreign currency funding.

4. Review the bank's contingency liquidity plan to ensure that it includes derivatives. This step should be coordinated with the examiner assigned to review "Liquidity." Determine if the plan:

    - Addresses potential market liquidity and cash flow funding aberrations for both on- and off-balance-sheet instruments.
    - Requires projections of cash flows (including asset usage from credit enhancements) under normal and stressed market conditions. Individual bank and system liquidity

crises should be projected.

- Assigns specific duties and responsibilities to individuals to manage derivatives in the event of deteriorating, as well as crisis, situations.
- Addresses the impact of collateral requirements and early termination requests.

Objective: To determine the adequacy of processes relating to management of foreign currency translation risk in derivatives activities.

1. Review the bank's systems to determine the timeliness and completeness of the information used to make cross-border investing and hedging decisions.

Objective: To determine the adequacy of processes relating to management of credit risk in derivatives activities.

1. Evaluate the process for determining whether a derivatives transaction is appropriate for the counterparty. Select a sample of recent derivatives transactions. The sample should focus on nondealer counterparties and include:

    - Contracts with large mark-to-market values (both positive and negative).
    - Complex, leveraged, and plain vanilla transactions.
    - Off-market, extended, or terminated transactions.

2. Review both the credit and marketing files for sample transactions to assess the adequacy of documentation relating to determining appropriateness. Discuss the sampled transaction with the responsible credit and/or marketing officers. Determine if:

    - Credit files contain sufficient information to understand the risks the customer is attempting to manage, types of derivatives expected to be used, and the overall impact on the customer.

- Marketing files contain information on the transaction and any disclosures given to the customer (e.g., customer profile information, deal term sheets, sales presentations, scenario analysis, correspondence).

3. Evaluate the adequacy of the credit risk measurement method used to calculate presettlement credit exposure through review of model information and discussions with management. Determine if:

- The system produces a reasonable estimate of loan-equivalent exposure including the current exposure (mark-to-market) plus an estimate of the potential change in value over the remaining life of the contract (add-on).
- The credit risk add-on calculation is:
  - Statistically derived from market factors.
  - Consistent with the probability modeling used to evaluate price risk, except that the add-on calculation will use the remaining life of the contract as a time horizon.
  - Based on peak exposure.
- The frequency of credit calculations is adequate.
- The bank maintains documentation to support that the assumptions used in the credit risk exposure calculation are updated as appropriate.

4. Review the credit risk measurement method used to calculate settlement exposure, and determine that it provides a reasonable estimate of risk.

5. Determine the degree to which the credit risk measurement system can aggregate credit exposure, on both a gross and net basis, across desks, branches, and/or globally.

6. Determine the extent to which management uses settlement, closeout, or multilateral netting arrangements. Determine:

- Whether the bank's operational systems can accommodate netting.
- Whether counterparty payments or credit exposures are netted for purposes of computing periodic settlement or reporting aggregate credit exposures.
- The process whereby management ensures that a signed master agreement is on file before netting is performed. Evaluate the bank's system to track and resolve unsigned master agreements.

7. Select a sample of counterparties where credit exposure is netted. Trace to supporting master agreements to ensure that each counterparty with which management nets exposure for risk management purposes has signed a master agreement.

8. Obtain a list of recent credit limit and policy exceptions. Determine whether the exceptions were identified and approved. Determine whether the basis and timeliness of approval was reasonable and within the approver's authority. Evaluate the level and nature of the exceptions.

9. Determine how the credit risk control function notifies traders of deteriorating trends in a counterparty's financial condition or changes in limits. Also determine how traders communicate their knowledge of counterparties' deteriorating financial condition to the credit risk control function.

10. Determine whether there have been any recent counterparty credit downgrades or deteriorations affecting the bank's trading activities. If so, determine the bank's response.

11. Determine how the bank identifies and reports past-due counterparty payments. Review the bank's past due, watch list, or deteriorating trend reports. Discuss management's workout strategy for these counterparties.

12. Determine whether the bank maintains credit reserves for counterparty exposures apart from the allowance for loan losses. Determine whether the method for calculating the reserves is reasonable.

13. Determine whether appropriate bank personnel have reviewed the counterparty's agreement with the investment advisor to assess the type of activities that are authorized or prohibited.

14. Determine whether senior management and credit risk management have assessed credit risk exposure arising from relationships with undisclosed counterparties. If so, evaluate their assessment and management's response.

15. Ensure that the process for approving, allocating, and reporting a breach of credit limits is adequate. Determine if:

    - Counterparty limits and transactions that exceed limits are monitored and approved by credit officers independent of trading personnel.
    - Traders have access to systems to ensure line availability (within presettlement, settlement, and tenor limits) before executing a transaction.
    - Traders are prohibited from trading with customers for whom no limits have been established except under specified conditions.
    - Written approvals are obtained for a breach of limits.
    - Customer positions are monitored to determine the impact that changing market rates could have on the counterparty's ability or willingness to fulfill the contract.

16. If the bank uses credit enhancements, margin arrangements, and third-party guarantees, determine that:

    - Controls are in place to limit and monitor use of these arrangements.

- These arrangements are not being used to take inappropriate risk positions.

Objective: To determine the adequacy of processes relating to management of transaction risk in derivatives activities.

1. Determine the responsibilities of the front, middle (if applicable), and back office in transaction processing.

2. Determine whether exception reports are provided to the appropriate level of management.

3. Evaluate the operations unit's ability to identify unusual transactions. Determine the systems designed to identify:

    - Off-premise trades.
    - After-hour trades.
    - Off-market trades.

4. Review a recent revaluation report for the derivatives portfolio. Determine the process (e.g., bid/offer, LOCOM, mid-market less adjustments) used by the bank to revalue the derivatives portfolio. Determine whether the approach is consistent with the liquidity and complexity of contracts (e.g., illiquid instruments may call for a more conservative valuation approach) and the sophistication of valuation and accounting systems.

5. For illiquid products for which independent quotes are not obtained, ask the bank to provide documentation supporting how the value was derived.

6. If the bank uses mid-market valuations, determine the extent and nature of valuation adjustments (e.g., credit, administrative, closeout costs, funding/investing costs, model errors) established at transaction inception. Determine

whether the bank justifies why certain adjustments listed above are not used. Determine whether adjustments are:

- Reasonable and well supported.
- Clearly authorized in policies and procedures.
- Consistently applied.
- Periodically reviewed for reasonableness.

7. Determine how discrepancies between front and back office comparisons are resolved. Select a sample from the larger discrepancies and determine the reason for each discrepancy and the final resolution.

8. Review the adequacy of the disaster recovery plan. Determine that:

- The plan is comprehensive, includes all critical support functions, and is periodically tested.
- The plan has been updated at least annually and incorporates market, product, and systems changes.

Objective: To determine the effectiveness of internal operating controls for derivatives activities.

1. Review the flow chart of front, middle, and back office systems configuration and identify important risk points. Evaluate the adequacy of the segregation of duties.

2. Assess the risk of errors and omissions by determining the degree in which various systems interface and the level of manual intervention required.

3. Determine if the back office (operating and accounting function) is functionally independent of the front office. Determine if the back office reports to a senior financial or operations manager and not to the risk-taker.

4. Review the reconciling process between general ledger and

operational databases, regulatory reports, and broker statements and between the front and back offices. Ensure that the person(s) who reconciles accounts does not also input transaction data. Consider the following:

- The frequency and volume of reconciling items.
- The process for sign-off on reconciliation differences.
- Whether senior managers review large reconciliation differences.

5.   Determine whether the derivatives valuation process is performed independently of the risk-takers and with appropriate frequency.

6.   Determine the quality of controls over the trade entry and processing environment. Controls should:

- Limit access to trading systems using passwords or similar controls.
- Ensure that all trades are captured through the use of:
  - Pre-numbered tickets or sequential numbering systems.
  - Recorded telephone conversations.
  - Chronological records of telex/SWIFT messages.
- Ensure that transaction documentation supports the reporting of limit exceptions. Ensure that records of original entry capture sufficient details to establish valid contracts, including:
  - Time and date executed.
  - Name of party executing transactions.
  - Name of party entering transaction data.
  - Type of instrument, price, and amount.
  - Adequate description of the components of complex transactions.
  - Settlement or effective date.
  - Payment or settlement instructions.
  - Brokers' fees or commissions and other expenses.

- Reduce the likelihood of errors by reconciling individual traders' positions/blotters to aggregate positions daily:
    - Front office to back office.
    - Aggregate position by instrument.
    - Customer/counterparty records.
- Safeguard assets by establishing controls over movement of cash, collateral, or other assets.
- Facilitate tracking and correction of errors through use of management information systems that monitor errors introduced by:
    - The party executing the trade.
    - The party entering the trade.
    - The settlement agent.

7. Determine if traders are prohibited from changing the terms of a transaction after they have orally committed to it.

8. Determine if the phone lines of traders and salespeople are taped. Determine also that the recordings are stored long enough to be used for resolving possible disputes.

9. Determine if controls over the confirmation process are sufficient. Determine if:

    - The back office initiates, follows up on, and controls the confirmation process.
    - Outgoing confirmations are initiated no later than one business day after the transaction date.
    - The method of confirmation used provides a documentation trail that supports the bank's position in the event of disputes (recorded telephone lines, paper confirmation, telex/SWIFT messages, logs of other contacts).
    - Outgoing confirmations are sent to the attention of a department at the counterparty that is independent of the trading unit.
    - Outgoing confirmations contain all relevant contract details.
    - Persons independent of the employees who execute trades handle incoming confirmations.

- Information on incoming confirmations is compared with outgoing information.
- All discrepancies requiring corrective action are promptly identified and followed up on by an independent party.
- All discrepancies (including outstanding confirmations) are tracked, dated, and reported to management. Trends by type are identified and addressed.
- The back office compares, for consistency, a deal's particulars (as evidenced in confirmations) with its earlier oral terms.

10. Review the settlement process and controls to ensure that they adequately limit settlement risk. Review the various methods of settlement (e.g., gross, net, DVP) for the range of products covered and note any exceptions to commonly accepted practices. Determine:

- If the bank has a process to individually track large transactions from commitment to settlement.
- To what extent the measurement of settlement risk takes into account the instances beyond which payments cannot be called back.
- Whether the bank uses standardized settlement instructions. Determine if changes to standard settlement instructions are properly controlled.
- If there is a review of nostro accounts to determine whether there are old outstanding items that could indicate settlement errors or poor procedures.
- Whether disbursements/receipts have been recalculated to reflect the net amounts for legally binding netting arrangements.
- If aging schedules are prepared to track outstanding settlement items and distributed to the appropriate level of operations and trading management.

11. Determine that back office controls over the release of funds

(payments, margin, and collateral) ensure that the person responsible for the release of funds is independent of confirmation responsibilities and sensitive operations processing duties.

12. Determine if persons who do not have trading authority make general ledger entries and reconciliations.

13. Determine if controls over the documentation tracking process ensure:

- Timely identification of missing documents.
- An organized follow-up process for obtaining missing documents.
- Timely resolution of documentation exceptions.
- That documentation exception reports are provided to operations and trading management.

14. Determine if a tickler system been established to:

- Ensure timely payments to the counterparty.
- Monitor and follow up on late payments.

15. Determine if controls over the back office revaluation process ensure that:

- Key pricing parameters are obtained from or verified by a source independent of the traders and are representative of the market.
- If rates are reset manually, there is a tickler system to prompt such action.
- Rate resets are verified for accuracy.
- For dealers, revaluations are performed daily.
- Profits and losses resulting from revaluations are closed to the general ledger at least once a month.
- If models are used to derive or interpolate specific market factors, the models have been independently reviewed or otherwise validated.

- If positions in thinly traded or illiquid portfolios are marked to model, the model is controlled by operations and that market factors (volatility, yield curves, etc.) are obtained from an independent source.

16. Determine if controls over the resolution of trade discrepancies ensure that:

- Someone resolves trade disputes other than the person who executed the contract.
- Trade discrepancies are brought to the immediate attention of the operations manager.
- Discrepancy documentation contains the key financial terms of the transaction, indicates the disputed item, and summarizes the resolution.
- The counterparty receives notice of the final disposition of the trade.
- The level and frequency of disputed trades is reasonable.

17. Determine if controls over the payment of broker commissions and fees ensure that:

- The back office reviews broker's statements, reconciles charges to bank estimates, checks commissions, and initiates payment.
- There is a mechanism to report unusual trends or charges to back office management.
- Brokerage activity is spread over a reasonable number of brokers and there is no evidence of favoritism.

18. If applicable, determine whether there is an adequate system to control collateral for derivatives transactions. Determine whether:

- Trading personnel are prohibited access to collateral or collateral records.

- Collateral is physically safeguarded and kept under dual control to prevent loss, unauthorized disposal, or use.
- Collateral is verified periodically, reconciled to the collateral record, and the results reported to management.
- Collateral is periodically revalued and compared to mark-to-market exposures.

19. Determine if controls over collateral in the custody of others ensure that:

- Collateral statements from brokers and other dealers are sent to the back office (or other appropriate department independent of the trading area), reconciled promptly, and differences investigated.
- Trading personnel are prevented from authorizing release of collateral.

20. Determine if policies and controls regarding the use of personal computers, including spreadsheet applications, ensure that:

- Traders cannot make changes to key spreadsheets for valuation or risk management purposes.
- Data and applications are protected.

21. If multiple databases are used to support subsidiary systems, determine if there are reconciliation controls at each point that multiple data files are brought together.

22. Determine if controls for tracking documentation exceptions ensure that:

- A comprehensive record of documentation exceptions is maintained.
- Efforts to clear documentation exceptions are adequate.
- Exceptions are tracked independently of approving officers.

Objective: To determine the adequacy of processes relating to management of compliance risk in derivatives activities.

1. Evaluate the adequacy of legal documentation tracking systems.

2. Determine that the bank requires legal opinions from all relevant jurisdictions addressing enforceability of a netting agreement before relying on the netting agreement to calculate and monitor credit exposure to the counterparty.

3. Determine that the bank adequately ensures that counterparties have the legal capacity to execute specific derivatives transactions.

4. Determine whether the bank's legal counsel has reviewed all agreements with investment advisors or other third-party intermediaries, including the representation and warranty agreements, to assess if the advisor's responsibilities are adequately defined.

Objective: To determine the adequacy of processes relating to management of reputation risk in derivatives activities.

1. Determine that business managers have developed contingency plans that describe actions to be taken in times of market disruption and major credit deteriorations to minimize losses and potential damage to the institution's market-making reputation.

2. Determine if there is a mechanism to promote awareness of the bank's code of ethics/conflict of interest policies. Determine if trading and sales personnel are required to confirm in writing their acknowledgment of various codes and to report violations.

Objective: To determine the adequacy of processes relating to management of strategic risk in derivatives activities.

1. Select a new product recently developed or transacted. Test compliance with the bank's new-product policy. Determine that the bank's new product definition adequately ensures reasonable new product discipline.

2. Evaluate the process the bank uses to ensure adequate capital is allocated to the derivatives business. Determine:

    •   If the board or appropriate senior management has approved the capital allocation process.
    •   If significant changes in derivatives activities triggers an analysis and affirmation of the adequacy of capital allocations.
    •   That all derivatives activities are incorporated into the bank's minimum regulatory capital calculations.

Personnel

Conclusion: Given the size and complexity of the bank, management and personnel (do, do not) possess the required skills and knowledge to effectively manage derivatives activities.

Objective: To evaluate the capabilities of key personnel regarding derivatives activities.

1. Determine whether management is technically qualified and capable of properly engaging in the derivatives activities transacted by the bank. Consider the following:

    •   Brief biographies of managers of units responsible for derivatives products.
    •   Job descriptions for key positions.

2. Review staffing levels, educational background, and work experience of the staff. Determine whether the bank has

sufficient and qualified staff to accommodate present and projected volumes and types of derivatives transactions.

3. Through discussions with credit risk control personnel, relationship managers, and loan review personnel evaluate their demonstrated knowledge of the products traded by the bank and understanding of current and potential credit exposure. Determine whether credit risk management staff demonstrate an ability to control and limit positions with counterparties.

4. Review compensation plans, including incentive components, for applicable derivatives staff (e.g., traders, salespeople, risk control, operations). Determine if the plans:

   - Are designed to recruit, develop, and retain appropriate talent.
   - Do not encourage employees to take risk that is incompatible with the bank's risk appetite or prevailing rules or regulations.
   - Are consistent with the long-term strategic goals of the bank.
   - Do not encourage sales practices that might damage the reputation of the bank.
   - Include compliance with bank policies, laws, and regulations.
   - Consider performance relative to the bank's stated goals.
   - Consider risk-adjusted return.
   - Consider competitors' compensation packages for similar responsibilities and performance.
   - Consider individual overall performance.

5. Determine whether the board holds management accountable for performance. Consider the following:

   - The consistency of performance against strategic and

financial objectives over time.
- Internal/external audit and regulatory examination results.
- The level of compliance with policies and procedures.

Controls

Conclusion: Management and the board (have, have not) implemented effective control systems for derivatives activities.

Objective: To determine the adequacy of internal or external audit coverage of derivatives activities.

1. Review the audit scope and frequency of the audits of derivatives activities. Determine if the audit scope includes:

    - Periodic review of the adequacy of all bank policies and procedures.
    - Periodic testing of compliance with policy, including risk limits.
    - Evaluation of the effectiveness and independence of the risk management process.
    - Ensuring the performance of an independent validation of the accuracy of pricing, revaluation, and risk measurement methodologies (including spreadsheet applications), with emphasis on new products.
    - Testing the reliability and timeliness of information reported to senior management and the board.
    - Evaluation of the adequacy of internal controls and the testing of operations functions including:
        - Segregation of duties.
        - Trade entry and transaction documentation.
        - Confirmations.
        - Settlement.
        - Cash management.
        - Revaluations.
        - Accounting treatment.
        - Independence and timeliness of the reconciliation processes.

- Assessment of the adequacy of data processing systems and software.
- Assessment of unusual situations such as off-market deals, unusual changes in volume, and after-hours and off-premises trading.
- Review of brokerage commissions and fees.
- Testing of trader and sales representatives' compensation calculations.
- Sampling credit files to ensure compliance with policies and procedures regarding documentation and appropriateness.
- Sampling marketing files to ensure compliance with policies and procedures regarding documentation and appropriateness.
- Ensuring that sales presentations are clear, balanced, and reasonable.
- Reviewing marketers' trading tapes to ensure propriety of sales discussions.

Reviewing transactions with undisclosed counterparties.

2. Assess the effectiveness of the audit process in ensuring internal controls are maintained and systems remain reliable. Review the findings of audits performed since the previous examination. Evaluate:

- Material criticisms or deficiencies.
- Timely implementation of corrective action.
- Quality of reporting to senior management and the board.

3. Determine adequacy of the audit staff size and qualifications. Consider independence, product complexity, and technical and systems skills.

4. Evaluate the bank/company's compliance program.

Determine:

- Responsibilities.
- Independence.
- Monitoring.
- Reporting.
- Ability to effect corrective action.

5.   Determine if there is a mechanism to ensure compliance with the code of ethics/conflict of interest policy and report violations.

Objective: To determine the adequacy of the independent risk control function.

1.   Determine that the board, through the ALCO or other appropriate policy forum, has established an independent price risk control function. Review the risk control function's role and structure. Determine if the risk control function:

- Reports independently from those individuals directly responsible for trading decisions and trading management.
- Is adequately staffed with qualified individuals.
- Is fully supported by the board and senior management and has sufficient stature within the organization to be effective.
- Has been provided with the technical and financial resources, corporate visibility, and authority to ensure effective oversight.

2.   Evaluate the organizational structure and staffing of the credit risk control function. Determine that:

- The credit risk control function reports independently of traders and marketers.
- Credit risk control personnel have sufficient authority to question traders' and marketers' decisions (e.g., appropriateness issues).

• The credit risk control function participates in the new-product approval process.

Objective: To determine the adequacy of the tools and information systems used to manage derivatives activities.

1. Review abstracted minutes of the board of directors meetings and other appropriate committee minutes such as ALCO, audit, and new products to determine the extent of oversight of derivatives activities.

2. Review information provided to the board and senior management. Determine whether the board and senior management have been provided with material sufficient to understand the bank's financial derivatives activities. This material should include:

  • A clear statement of derivatives strategy and performance relative to objectives, including a periodic analysis of risk-adjusted return.
  • Ongoing educational material and information regarding major activities.
  • Reports indicating compliance with policies and law, including OCC policy.
  • Internal and external audit reports.
  • Reports indicating level of risk.
  • Reports attesting to the validation/quality of risk measurement systems.
  • Reports indicating the sufficiency of internal controls.
  • Reports detailing performance of trading activity.
  • Other pertinent information.

3. Determine how management communicates price risk exposure to appropriate levels within the organization. Refer to the list of standard reports in the "Price Risk" section of the

narrative that management should generate to properly communicate price risk exposure. The formality and frequency of reporting should be directly related to the level of derivatives activities and risk exposure.

4. Review price risk monitoring reports used by management (e.g., sources, levels and trends of price risk, compliance with policy). Determine if the reports include all significant sources of price risk.

5. Determine whether management has documented and supported the price risk measurement method and the underlying assumptions. Consider the following:

    -   Board or senior management approval of quantitative methodology.
    -   Annual reporting to senior management that discusses both the benefits and the limitations of the methodologies and systems chosen relative to the characteristics of the existing activity.
    -   For VAR models, the following assumptions should be documented:
        -   Data series.
        -   Confidence intervals.
        -   Holding periods.
        -   Source of information used to construct databases.
        -   Correlation calculations and application.
        -   Source of volatility factors.
        -   Frequency of database update.

6. Determine whether management performs back-testing of the price risk measurement model, comparing risk measurement results against actual daily profits and losses. If so, evaluate the results of back-testing and analyses of the causes of material differences. If back-testing is not performed, determine whether it should be conducted.

7. Determine whether management recalibrates pricing models

periodically by comparing the theoretical value of an instrument to actual market prices. Determine whether material differences have been effectively addressed.

8. Determine whether key pricing, revaluation, and risk measurement models have been appropriately validated. Determine if the validation:

- Incorporates all relevant systems, including spreadsheet applications.
- Is performed by a competent party independent of the business using or generating the model.
- Has been adequately documented.
- Is performed before the model is put into regular use and periodically thereafter as market conditions warrant (e.g., unusual market volatility may trigger a re-validation).
- Includes an evaluation of routines to convert underlying position data to the format required by the models.
- Management has reviewed results.

9. Determine whether the liquidity risks posed by derivatives activities are factored into liquidity-related management information systems (MIS). Ensure that MIS provide appropriate analytical information and early warning. Determine if liquidity reports include:

- Projected cash flows from on- and off-balance-sheet instruments, including foreign currency requirements. Projections should be sufficiently long term to capture all material maturities and cash flows.
- Current mark-to-market data.
- Counterparty exposures.
- Concentrations within markets, instruments, maturities and customers.
- Current and expected impact of credit enhancements.
- Other information that should be available if necessary:

    – Changes in counterparty line availability.
    – Changes in bid/ask spreads.
    – Increasing demands for collateral or early terminations, suggesting an adverse perception of the bank by the market.

10.   Determine how management communicates credit risk exposure to appropriate levels within the organization. Determine whether the reports are generated independently and are provided to the various levels of management and the board. Refer to the list of standard reports (in the section of the narrative on credit risk) management should generate to properly communicate credit risk exposures. The formality and frequency of reporting should be directly related to the level of derivatives activities and risk exposure.

11.   Determine whether the credit risk measurement methodology has been independently validated prior to its first use and at least annually thereafter, or as market conditions warrant. Determine if:

    •   The validation process incorporates all relevant systems, including spreadsheet applications.
    •   A competent party independent of the business line using or generating the model performs the validation.
    •   The validation process has been adequately documented.
    •   The validation includes an evaluation of routines to convert underlying position data to the format required by the system.
    •   Management has adequately responded to validation results.

12.   Determine if the operations unit generates management reports that reflect current status and trends. These reports should include:

    •   Aging of documentation exceptions.

- Position reconcilements.
- Outstanding general ledger reconciling items.
- Failed trades.
- After-hour and off-premise trades.
- Off-market trades.
- Aging of unconfirmed trades.
- Suspense items payable/receivable.
- Brokerage payments.
- Miscellaneous losses.

Note: The content and frequency of reports will vary but the bank must be able to track errors and miscellaneous losses in sufficient detail to pinpoint the source of problems. Reports provided to senior management should be prepared independent of traders.

Active Position-Takers and Limited End Users

Quantity of Risk

Conclusion: The quantity of risk is (low, moderate, high).

Objective: To determine the quantity of interest rate risk resulting from derivatives activities.

1. Evaluate the impact of interest rate volatility on earnings. Review budget and budget variance reports for the past 12 months focusing on earnings. Discuss significant budget variances with management.

2. Assess the volatility of earnings over time. Review any written explanation of earnings performance. Consider actual earnings performance against budgeted earnings and overall levels of risk taken.

3. Assess the current level of interest rate risk (e.g., earnings- and EVE-at-risk) against capital and earnings.

4. Review the reasonableness of interest rate earnings-at-risk limits relative to budgeted earnings.

For banks investing in structured notes:

5. Assess the interest rate risk of structured note investments. Consider the following:

    *   Maturities of assets.
    *   Results of any market value stress tests available in the bank's files.
    *   Use of notes with leverage (multipliers greater than one) or variable principal redemption.
    *   Amount of structured note holdings relative to the bank's capital.
    *   Management's ability to understand the risks of the notes.

6. Verify that the bank's portfolio contains current and accurate prices for structured notes. Ensure any write-downs for available-for-sale securities have been taken.

Objective: To determine the quantity of liquidity risk resulting from derivatives activities.

1. Evaluate the bank's use of credit enhancements, margin arrangements, and third-party guarantees and their impact on the level of liquidity risk. Determine that these arrangements are not being used to take inappropriate risk positions.

2. Evaluate the bank's the use of early termination triggers and their impact on the level of liquidity risk.

3. As appropriate for the nature and complexity of the bank's activities, consider the following and their impact on the level of liquidity risk:

    - Management is able to adequately measure and predict cash flow, collateral, and liquidity needs.
    - Good communication exists between derivatives managers and persons responsible for funding.
    - When derivatives activity is material, contingency funding plans and liquidity information systems formally incorporate derivatives activity.
    - If applicable, policy issues involving collateral and margin arrangements and risks associated with early termination requests have been considered.
    - Management information systems adequately depict:
        - Impact of derivatives on overall liquidity and projected sources and uses of funds.
        - Current and expected impact of credit enhancements on liquidity.
        - Current mark-to-market data.

Objective: To determine the quantity of credit risk resulting from derivatives activities.

1. Evaluate the level of credit risk with derivatives counterparties. Select a sample of counterparties from the list of derivatives counterparties. Review credit files for the sample counterparties. Determine if:

   - Files are current and contain sufficient information to document an informed credit decision, including purpose, source of repayment, and collateral.
   - Credit evaluations aggregate limits for derivatives with the limits established for other activities, including commercial lending.
   - Distinct limits are established for settlement and presettlement risk and are well supported.
   - Risk ratings are accurate and supported.

2. Determine how the bank identifies and reports past-due counterparty payments. Review the bank's past-due, watch list, or deteriorating trend reports. Discuss management's workout strategy for these counterparties.

Objective: To determine the quantity of transaction risk resulting from derivatives activities.

1. Evaluate the adequacy of operations support, including systems adequacy, in light of the level of current and expected trading volume and complexity of transactions.

2. Review exception reports on operations (e.g., aging, failed trades, off-market trades, outstanding items, suspense items, and miscellaneous losses). Evaluate the level and nature of exceptions. Determine whether appropriate approval was obtained when warranted. Determine whether exception reports are sent to the appropriate level of management.

3.   Review the disaster recovery plan. Determine whether:

- The plan is comprehensive and includes all critical support functions.
- The plan has been tested periodically.
- The plan has been updated at least annually and incorporates market, product, and systems changes.

Objective: To determine the quantity of compliance risk resulting from derivatives activities.

1.   Review legal documentation exception reports. Evaluate the adequacy of tracking systems. Evaluate the source, nature, and level of exceptions.

2.   Discuss with management any pending litigation or complaints lodged against a counterparty relating to derivatives activities. Evaluate the source, nature, and level of litigation/complaints.

3.   Verify that the bank is reporting derivatives transactions consistent with call report instructions.

Objective: To determine the quantity of strategic risk resulting from derivatives activities.

1.   Review and discuss future plans and strategies relating to the bank's use of derivatives with management. Focus on the following:

- Positioning and hedging strategies.
- New system or model upgrades.
- Anticipated changes in the risk profile.

2.   Select a sample of derivatives transactions initiated over the past 12 months. Determine whether the strategy behind the

transaction is well documented and consistent with the bank's overall business and strategic plans. For hedging transactions, determine that standards for hedge effectiveness have been established.

Objective: To determine the quantity of reputation risk resulting from derivatives activities.

1.   Determine the credit rating and market acceptance of the bank as a counterparty in the markets. If the bank recently experienced a rating downgrade, ascertain the impact (e.g., counterparties report they are full up or decline long-dated transactions, calls for collateral, or early termination).

Active Position-Takers and Limited End Users

Quality of Risk Management

Conclusion: **The quality of risk management is (strong, satisfactory, weak).**

Policy

Conclusion: The board (has, has not) established effective policies relating to the bank's derivatives activities.

Objective: To determine if policies adequately address use of derivatives as investment substitutes or risk management tools.

1. Evaluate the adequacy of policies with respect to use of derivatives as investment substitutes or risk management tools. Determine if they:

   - Authorize the use of derivatives.
   - Address overall net income and capital objectives.
   - Require analysis that reflects the expected impact of derivatives on the overall interest rate risk profile in terms of earnings-at-risk or economic value.
   - Require the periodic testing of interest rate risk positions and the derivatives cash flows under adverse changes in interest rates and other market conditions.
   - Describe which derivatives instruments are authorized. Determine that the approval process considers:
     - The liquidity of the instrument.
     - Leverage.
     - The capacity and creditworthiness of approved counterparties.
     - The ability of interest rate risk models to evaluate the derivatives instruments.
   - Require that derivatives be independently revalued for

---

risk control purposes.
- Require outside price sources be used where appropriate.
- Establish, in the absence of authoritative accounting guidance, hedge accounting criteria, including ongoing testing of hedging effectiveness.
- Detail appropriate accounting procedures.
- Require annual board approval.

For banks investing in structured notes:

2. Determine whether the investment policy allows the purchase of structured notes that are leveraged or whose principal redemption amount is based on a formula. These types of structured notes generally have more risk and should be explicitly authorized by policy.

3. Determine whether the bank has established limits for the degree of interest rate risk acceptable for structured notes and other investment securities.

4. Review the bank's policies with respect to secondary market purchases and sales of structured notes to determine whether the bank obtains price quotations from several firms to ensure fair prices.

Objective: To determine the adequacy of derivatives policies relating to liquidity risk management activities.

1. Evaluate the adequacy of liquidity risk management policies and procedures. Determine if they:

    - Require that liquidity-related management information systems and contingency plans address derivatives and corresponding collateral, margin arrangements, and early termination agreements when such activities are material.
    - Detail circumstances in which the bank will honor noncontractual early termination requests.

- Provide guidance on the use of credit enhancements.
- Limit the amount of assets that can be encumbered by collateral and margin arrangements. (Such limits are generally determined after performing analyses to identify requirements under adverse scenarios.)
- Limit the amount of collateral tied to common triggers (e.g., credit rating).
- Require annual board approval.

Objective: To determine the adequacy of derivatives policies relating to credit risk management activities.

1. Evaluate the adequacy of credit risk policies and procedures with respect to use of derivatives as investment substitutes or risk management tools. Determine if the policies:

- Establish guidelines for derivatives portfolio credit quality, concentrations, and tenors.
- Require periodic counterparty review and assignment of risk ratings.
- Prescribe the method of calculating counterparty credit risk exposure.
- Establish and define formal reporting requirements on counterparty credit exposure.
- Require designation of separate counterparty limits for presettlement and settlement credit risk.
- Require independent monitoring and reporting of aggregate credit exposure for each counterparty (including all credit exposure arising in other business lines) and comparison with limits.
- Describe the mechanism for policy and limit exception approvals and reporting.
- Outline what to do when a limit on a counterparty credit line is exceeded because of a large market move (e.g., collateral calls, up-front payments, termination).
- Require annual board approval.

2.   Determine if the bank's procedures and written agreements regarding the use of credit enhancements and early termination clauses address:

- Evaluating the counterparty's ability to provide and meet collateral or margin requirements at inception and during the term of the agreement.
- Acceptable types of instruments for collateral and margin.
- Ability to substitute assets.
- Time of posting (i.e., at inception, upon change in risk rating, upon change in level of exposure).
- Valuation methods (i.e., sources of pricing, timing of revaluation).
- Ability to hypothecate contracts.
- Physical control over assets.

Objective: To determine the adequacy of derivatives policies relating to transaction risk management activities.

1.   Evaluate the adequacy of operational policies and procedures. Determine if they address:

- Segregation of duties between trading, processing, and payment functions.
- Description of accounts.
- Trade entry and transaction documentation.
- Confirmations.
- Settlement.
- Exception reporting.
- Documentation tracking and reporting.
- Revaluation.
- Reconciliations including frequency.
- Discrepancies and disputed trades.
- Broker accounts.
- Accounting treatment.
- Management reporting.

Objective: To determine the adequacy of derivatives policies relating to compliance risk management activities.

1. Ensure that policies require appropriate legal review for new products, counterparty or agreement forms, and netting arrangements.

2. Obtain a copy of the hedge accounting policies and review for conformance with authoritative pronouncements by the Financial Accounting Standards Board and call report instructions.

3. In the absence of authoritative accounting guidance, determine whether the accounting policy for derivatives transactions is reasonable and consistently applied.

Objective: To determine the adequacy of derivatives policies relating to reputation risk management activities.

1. If the bank uses derivatives in a fiduciary capacity, determine whether appropriate policies and procedures are in place to ensure effective risk management. (Refer to OCC Bulletin 96-25, "Fiduciary Risk Management of Derivatives and Mortgage-backed Securities.")

Processes

Conclusion: Management and the board (have, have not) implemented effective processes to manage derivatives activities.

Objective: To determine the effectiveness of processes relating to management of interest rate risk in derivatives activities.

1. Review the bank's historical interest rate risk against limits.

Determine limit exceptions were properly approved and documented.

2.   Evaluate the manner in which positioning/hedging activities are formulated, executed, and monitored. Consider the following:

- Line management's day-to-day oversight of positioning/hedging activities.
- The limits of and restrictions on delegated authorities.
- Requirements for approving transactions in new products, markets, and extended maturities.
- Management's authority and willingness to modify or override a risk-taker's decisions (using offsetting positions or specific instructions).
- Senior management oversight.
- Modifications of strategies and activities in varying market conditions.

3.   Determine the bank's process for initiating a derivatives transaction. Discuss the number of counterparty quotes normally obtained and what price range the bank usually observes for each type of instrument used. Determine whether the bank relies on a dealer for advice. If so, determine whether there is an advisory agreement in place.

4.   Evaluate the method used to measure interest rate risk exposure. Determine who developed and maintains the system. Assess whether the method is commensurate with the nature and complexity of the activity conducted. Determine if:

- Interest rate risk is measured and managed on a legal entity or corporate basis.
- The bank's systems can aggregate interest rate risk exposure corporate-wide.
- Earnings-at-risk is reported for current interest rates, as well as movement up or down in interest rates.
- Economic value of equity is reported for banks with significant medium- to long-term positions.

- The exposure arising from a change in interest rates can be evaluated and reported in a timely manner.
- Management has documented and supported the risk measurement method and the underlying assumptions.

5. If the bank uses a interest rate risk simulation model, determine whether management:

- Performs stress tests. Evaluate the basis of the stress tests and determine whether the assumptions are reasonable.
- Performed any back-testing by comparing risk measurement results against actual profits and losses. Evaluate the results of the back-testing and reconcilement of differences.

6. For banks investing in structured notes, determine how management evaluates the degree of price sensitivity of structured notes (e.g., internally developing their own stress tests or relying on tests supplied by outside sources) and the impact on bank-wide asset/liability management risk profile. Consider:

- If management relies on stress tests supplied by outside sources, determine whether management understands the assumptions used in the tests and can explain the results.
- If management performs its own stress tests, evaluate the integrity of the data and management's ability to properly estimate risk.

Objective: To determine the effectiveness of processes relating to management of credit risk in derivatives activities.

1. Evaluate the process for underwriting counterparties. From the sample of derivatives counterparty credit files previously selected (for determining quantity of risk), determine if:

- Credit personnel independent of the interest rate risk management function have approved counterparties.
- Credit personnel have assessed the counterparty's ability to meet its obligations over the life of the contract.
- The bank has considered the counterparty's willingness and ability to meet servicing requirements (e.g., provide periodic mark-to-market values) and willingness to terminate an OTC transaction before maturity and at market value.

2. Obtain a list of recent credit limit and policy exceptions. Determine whether the exceptions were identified and approved in a timely manner. Determine whether the basis of approval was reasonable and within the approver's authority. Evaluate the level and nature of the exceptions.

3. Determine that the process for approving, allocating, and reporting breaches of credit limits ensures that:

- Counterparty limits and the exceeding of such limits are monitored and approved independently of the trading floor.
- Traders have access to systems to ensure line availability (within presettlement, settlement, and tenor limits) before executing a transaction.
- Traders are prohibited, except under specified conditions, from conducting transactions with counterparties for whom no limits have been established.
- Written approvals are obtained for any breach of limits.
- Net positions are monitored to determine the impact that changing market rates could have on the counterparty's ability or willingness to fulfill the contract.

4. Review the credit risk measurement method used for presettlement credit exposure. Consider:

- If the bank uses a model to calculate the credit risk exposure, determine that:
  - The system produces a reasonable estimate of loan equivalent exposure including the current exposure

(mark-to-market) plus an estimate of the potential change in value of the remaining life of the contract (add-on).

- The credit risk add-on calculation is statistically derived from market factors and is consistent with the probability modeling used, if any, to evaluate price risk (except that the add-on calculation will use time horizon of the remaining life of the contract) and based on peak exposure.
- The bank maintains documentation to support the assumptions used in the credit calculation and simulation analysis and that the assumptions used are kept current.

- If the bank uses closeout netting agreements, ensure that the add-ons are not netted against negative mark-to-markets.
- If the bank uses a non-statistically-based method (such as a general percentage of notional values), determine whether the bank uses other risk controls such as restricting transactions to high-quality counterparties, limiting the tenor of deals, prescribing less volatile derivatives, or using conservative risk factors.
- Determine whether credit calculations are sufficiently frequent.
- Determine whether the model has been reviewed and validated by an independent party.

5. Review the method of measuring settlement risk, and determine whether it is reasonable. Consider:

- The various methods of settlement (e.g., gross, net, DVP) for the range of products covered and note any exceptions to commonly accepted practices.
- Whether the bank has a process to individually track large transactions from commitment to settlement.
- Whether the bank uses standardized settlement instructions.

- Whether disbursements/receipts have been recalculated to reflect the net amounts for legally binding netting arrangements.

6. Select a sample of counterparty credit files. Review the process for approving and monitoring derivatives product counterparties. Determine if:

    - Credit personnel independent of the interest rate risk management function have approved counterparties.
    - Credit personnel have assessed the counterparty's ability to meet its obligations over the life of the contract.
    - The bank has considered the counterparty's willingness and ability to meet servicing requirements (e.g., provide periodic mark-to-market values) and willingness to terminate an OTC transaction before maturity and at market value.

7. Determine whether procedures are in place for actions to take if counterparty limits are exceeded because of large market moves (e.g., obtaining collateral, up-front payments, deal termination or restructure).

8. Coordinating with the examiner responsible for examining loan portfolio management, review the bank's credit administration procedures for assigning risk ratings, identifying nonperforming contracts and determining allowance allocations. Determine that the procedures are reasonable.

Objective: To determine the effectiveness of processes relating to management of transaction risk in derivatives activities.

1. From discussions with the credit operations department or another department ensure that:

    - The bank has sufficient capacity to run all transactions through the credit exposure model at reasonable intervals.
    - Credit exposure calculations are performed or verified by people independent of the trading function.

- Credit lines (including lines for presettlement, settlement, and tenor) and usage are updated and changed on the system in a timely manner.

2. Evaluate the bank's method of revaluing derivatives contracts. Consider:

   - If outside sources are used, determine whether the bank obtains several quotes, independent of the originating dealer.
   - If the bank revalues the position internally, determine whether the revaluation methodology is consistent with the volatility and complexity of the instruments.
   - Ensure that values are obtained independent of the risk-taker.
   - Ensure the revaluation is performed with reasonable frequency. Active position-takers should formally revalue positions at least monthly and should be able to obtain daily revaluations. Limited end-users should formally revalue derivatives at least quarterly but be able to obtain monthly revaluations.

3. Review the reconciling process between general ledger and operational databases, regulatory reports, and broker statements and between the front and back offices. Ensure that the person(s) responsible for performing the reconciliation of accounts is independent of inputting transaction data. Consider:

   - The frequency and volume of reconciling items.
   - The process for sign-off on reconciliation differences.
   - Whether senior managers review large reconciliation differences.

Objective: To determine the effectiveness of internal operating controls for derivatives activities

---

1. Determine that the back office (operation/accounting function) is functionally independent of the front office. Determine if the back office reports to senior financial or operations manager and not to the risk-taker.

2. Review controls over the confirmation process. Determine if:

    *   The back office initiates, follows up on, and controls the confirmation process.
    *   The method of confirmation provides a documentation trail that supports the bank's position in the event of disputes (recorded telephone lines, paper confirmation, telex/SWIFT messages, logs of other contacts).
    *   Persons independent of the employees who execute trades handle incoming confirmations.
    *   All discrepancies requiring corrective action are promptly identified and resolved by an independent party.
    *   All discrepancies (including outstanding confirmations) are tracked, aged, and reported to management. Trends by type are identified and addressed.
    *   The back office compares, for consistency, the terms of the written confirmation with those of the earlier oral agreement.

3. Review controls over the settlement process. Determine if:

    *   Standardized settlement instructions have been established where possible.
    *   Changes to standardized settlement instructions are properly controlled.
    *   Nostro accounts do not contain old or stale dated items.
    *   Aging schedules are prepared to track outstanding settlement items.
    *   Aging information is reported to the appropriate level of operations and trading management.
    *   Disbursements and receipts have been

recalculated to reflect the net amounts of legally binding netting arrangements.

4. Review back office controls over the release of funds (swap payments, margin, collateral) to ensure that the person responsible for the release of funds is independent of confirmation responsibilities and sensitive operational processing duties

5. Determine if persons who do not have trading authority make general ledger entries and reconciliations.

6. Review controls over the documentation tracking process. Determine whether:

   - Missing documents are identified in a timely manner.
   - The bank has an organized follow-up process for obtaining these missing documents.
   - Documentation exceptions are resolved in a timely manner.
   - Documentation exception reports are provided to operations and trading management.

7. Determine if a tickler system has been established to:

   - Ensure timely payments to the counterparty.
   - Monitor and follow up on late payments.

8. Review controls over the back office revaluation process. Determine whether:

   - Key pricing parameters are obtained from or verified by a source independent of the traders and are representative of the market.
   - There is a tickler system to prompt action, if rates are reset manually.
   - Rate resets are verified for accuracy.

- Active position-takers perform revaluations at least monthly and are able to do so daily. Limited end-users perform valuations at least quarterly and are able to do so monthly.
- Profits and losses resulting from revaluations are closed to the general ledger at least once a month.
- The models have been independently reviewed or otherwise validated, if models are used to derive or interpolate specific market factors.
- The model is controlled by operations and that market factors (volatility, yield curves, etc.) are obtained from an independent source, if positions in thinly traded or illiquid portfolios are marked to model.

9. Review controls over the resolution of trade discrepancies. Determine whether:

- Someone resolves trade disputes other than the person who executed the contract.
- Trade discrepancies are brought to the immediate attention of the operations manager.
- Discrepancy documentation contains the key financial terms of the transaction, indicates the disputed item, and summarizes the resolution.
- The counterparty is notified of the final disposition of the trade.
- The level and frequency of disputed trades is reasonable.

10. Review controls over the payment of broker commissions and fees. Determine if:

- The back office reviews broker's statements, reconciles charges to bank estimates, checks commissions, and initiates payment.
- There is a mechanism to report unusual trends or charges to back office management.
- Brokerage activity is spread over a reasonable number of brokers and there is no evidence of favoritism.

11.   If applicable, determine whether there is an adequate system to control collateral on derivatives transactions. Determine if:

- Risk taking personnel are prohibited access to collateral or collateral records.
- Collateral is physically safeguarded and kept under dual control to prevent loss, unauthorized disposal, or use.
- Collateral is counted frequently on an unannounced basis, reconciled to the collateral record, and the results reported to management.
- Collateral is periodically revalued and compared with mark-to-market exposures.

12.   Review controls over collateral in the custody of others. Determine if:

- Collateral statements from brokers and other dealers are sent to the back office (or other appropriate department independent of the risk taking area), reconciled promptly, and differences resolved.
- Risk taking personnel are prevented from authorizing release of collateral.

13.   Review controls regarding the use of personal computers, including spreadsheet applications. Consider:

- Risk taking personnel cannot make changes to key spreadsheets for valuation or risk management purposes.
- Data and applications are protected.

14.   If multiple databases are used to support subsidiary systems, determine if there are reconciliation controls at each point that multiple data files are brought together.

15.   Determine if the bank has the operational capacity to process,

confirm, and record derivatives transactions in a controlled environment. Consider:

- Transactions are processed and confirmed independently of the area that enters the transactions.
- If transactions are maintained on a personal computer spreadsheet, adequate controls safeguard the data.
- Revaluations are done at least monthly for MIS and risk control purposes.
- Prices for periodic market valuations are obtained or verified from a source independent of the area that enters into the transactions.
- Personnel who are independent of the transaction make general ledger entries.
- The persons who reconcile accounts are independent of risk-taking and confirmation duties.

Objective: To determine the effectiveness of processes relating to management of compliance risk in derivatives activities.

1.   Determine that the bank adequately ensures that counterparties have the legal capacity to execute specific derivatives transactions.

2.   Determine that the institution adequately documents the legality of the activity for a national bank. If the bank is required to notify the OCC and receive prior approval to engage in the activity, determine that such approval has been obtained.

3.   Ensure that the bank requires legal opinions from all relevant jurisdictions addressing enforceability of a netting agreement before relying on the netting agreement to calculate and monitor credit exposure to the counterparty.

Objective: To determine the effectiveness of processes relating to management of strategic risk in derivatives activities.

1. Evaluate the process the bank uses to ensure adequate capital is allocated to derivatives activities. Determine:

   - Whether significant changes in derivatives activities trigger an analysis and affirmation of the adequacy of capital allocations.
   - That all derivatives activities are accounted for in the bank's minimum regulatory capital calculations.

Personnel

Conclusion: Given the size and complexity of the bank, management and personnel (do, do not) possess the required skills and knowledge to effectively manage derivatives activities.

Objective: To evaluate the capabilities of key personnel regarding derivatives activities.

1. Determine whether management is technically qualified and capable of engaging in the derivatives activities being undertaken.

2. Determine whether the board holds management accountable for performance. Consider:

   - The consistency of performance against strategic and financial objectives over time.
   - Internal/external audit and regulatory examination results.
   - The level of compliance with policy, procedure, and limits.
   - The quality and timeliness of communication to the board.

Controls

Conclusion: Management and the board (have, have not)

implemented effective control systems for derivatives activities.

Objective: To determine the adequacy of internal or external audit of derivatives activities.

1. Review the audit scope and frequency of the audits of derivatives activities. Determine if the audit:

    •   Periodically reviews applicable bank policies, limits, internal controls, and procedures.
    •   Apprises the adequacy of accounting, operating, compliance, and risk management controls.
    •   Periodically tests compliance with policy, including risk limits.
    •   Samples credit files to ensure compliance with policies and procedures regarding documentation.
    •   Evaluates the effectiveness and independence of the risk management function.
    •   Verifies the accuracy of risk measurement and revaluation methodologies, if not performed by another independent party.
    •   Tests operational functions, including:
        –   Segregation of duties.
        –   Trade entry and transaction documentation.
        –   Confirmations.
        –   Settlement.
        –   Cash management.
        –   Revaluations.
        –   Accounting treatment.
        –   Independence and timeliness of the reconciliation processes.

2. Assess the effectiveness of the audit process in ensuring internal controls are maintained and systems remain reliable. Review the findings of audits performed since the previous examination. Evaluate:

    •   Material criticisms or deficiencies.

- Timely implementation of corrective action.
- Quality of reporting to senior management and the board.

3. Determine adequacy of the audit staff size and qualifications. Consider independence, product complexity, and technical and systems skills.

4. Evaluate the bank/company's compliance program. Determine:

   - Responsibilities.
   - Independence.
   - Monitoring.
   - Reporting.
   - Ability to effect corrective action.

Objective: To determine the adequacy of the independent risk control function.

1. Determine whether the board has established an interest rate risk control function. If so, review the oversight responsibility and staffing of the risk control function. In small banks, often the most practical solution is to use independent treasury support units or qualified outside consultants. Determine if the risk control function is:

   - Independent of persons directly responsible for entering into derivatives transactions.
   - Fully staffed with qualified individuals.
   - Fully supported by the board and senior management.
   - Provided with the technical and financial resources, organizational visibility, and authority necessary to ensure effective oversight.

2. Evaluate the organizational structure and staffing of the credit

risk control function. Determine if:

- The credit risk control function reports independently of risk takers.
- The credit risk control function participates in the new-product approval process.

Objective: To determine the adequacy of the tools and information systems used to manage derivatives activities.

1. Review abstracted minutes of the board of directors meetings and other appropriate committee minutes such as ALCO, audit, and new products to determine the extent of their oversight of derivatives activities.

2. Review material provided senior management and the board. Determine whether they have been provided with sufficient information to understand the bank's financial derivatives activities. This material should include:

- A clear statement of derivatives strategies and policies.
- Ongoing educational material and information.
- Reports indicating compliance with policy and law.
- Internal and external audit reports.
- Reports indicating the sufficiency of internal controls.
- Reports indicating the performance of positioning or hedging activity.
- Reports detailing interest rate sensitivity and the impact of derivatives transactions on earnings and capital. For active position-takers, this should include a periodic analysis of risk-adjusted return.
- Periodic reports showing the appreciation and depreciation of derivatives transactions.

3. Review interest rate risk management reports used by senior and line management with respect to derivatives and evaluate their comprehensiveness.

4. Review the effectiveness of the limit structure in view of interest rate management activities. Consider:

- Limits are consistent with articulated strategy.
- Limits are reasonable in light of end-user qualifications, recent profit and loss experience, budget expectations, and usage.
- Limits adequately control exposures to identified interest rate risk in normal and volatile market conditions.
- Limits are reassessed regularly and that appropriate revisions are made to reflect changes in strategies, staff, or market dynamics.

5. For hedge transactions, review hedge documentation to determine that:

- Hedging effectiveness is appropriately tested.
- Hedges are linked to identifiable exposures.
- The process used to determine correlation and the hedge ratio is reasonable.

6. Determine that key revaluation and interest rate risk measurement models have been validated. Evaluate the adequacy of the validation process. The validation process should:

- Incorporate all relevant systems, including spreadsheet applications.
- Be performed by a competent party independent of the business using or generating the model.
- Incorporate a qualitative review of data capture, the reasonableness and accuracy of assumptions, and data output.
- Have been adequately documented.
- Be performed prior to the model's regular use and periodically thereafter, as market conditions warrant.

7.   Determine if management has adequately responded to validation results.

8.   Determine how the bank communicates interest rate risk exposure to appropriate levels within the organization. Refer to the list of standard reports in the "Interest Rate Risk" narrative section that management should generate to properly communicate interest rate risk exposure. The formality and frequency of reporting should be directly related to the level of derivatives activities and risk exposure.

9.   Determine whether established limits adequately control the range of liquidity risks. Determine that the limits are appropriate for the level of activity.

10.   Determine how the bank communicates credit risk exposure to appropriate levels within the organization. Determine whether the reports are generated independently and are provided to the various levels of management and the board. Refer to the list of standard reports in the "Credit Risk" narrative section that management should generate to properly communicate credit risk exposures. The formality and frequency of reporting should be directly related to the level of derivatives activities and risk exposure.

Conclusion

Objective: To prepare written conclusion comments and communicate findings to management. Review findings with the EIC prior to discussion with management.

1. Provide the EIC with a conclusion memo that sufficiently addresses the quantity of all risks and quality of risk management.

2. Determine the impact on the aggregate and direction of risk assessments for any applicable risks identified by performing the above procedures. Examiners should refer to guidance provided under the OCC's large and community bank risk assessment programs.

   - Risk Categories: Compliance, Credit, Foreign Currency Translation, Interest Rate, Liquidity, Price,   Reputation, Strategic, Transaction
   - Risk Conclusions: High, Moderate, or Low
   - Risk Direction: Increasing, Stable, or Decreasing

3. Determine, in consultation with EIC, if the risks identified are significant enough to merit bringing them to the board's attention in the report of examination. If so, prepare items for inclusion under the heading Matters Requiring Board Attention. Consider:

   Considerations
   - MRBA should cover practices that:
     - Deviate from sound fundamental principles and are likely to result in financial deterioration if not addressed.
     - Result in substantive noncompliance with laws.
   - MRBA should discuss:
     - Causative factors contributing to the problem.
     - Consequences of inaction.

     – Management's commitment for corrective action.
     – The time frame and person(s) responsible for corrective action.

4. Discuss findings with management including conclusions regarding applicable risks, quality of risk management, aggregate risk, and direction of risk.

5. As appropriate, prepare a brief comment for inclusion in the report of examination.

6. Prepare a memorandum or update the work program with any information that will facilitate future examinations.

7. Update the OCC database and any applicable report of examination schedules or tables.

8. Organize and reference working papers in accordance with OCC guidance.

Risk Management of Financial Derivatives

Appendix A

Uniform Product Assessment

Below is a list of elements that a bank should include in its uniform product assessment:

- Product definition.

- Explanation of how the product or activity meets business strategies and objectives (e.g., customer service, risk management tool).

- Pricing mechanisms.

- Description of risk management processes.

- Descriptions of limits and exception approval processes.

- Capital allocations.

- Accounting procedures.

- Operating procedures and controls.

- Legal documentation requirements.

- Other legal and regulatory issues.

- Tax implications.

- Ongoing update/maintenance.

Risk Management
of Financial Derivatives

Appendix B

The "Greeks"

The "Greeks" that follow are the primary measures of options sensitivity.

Delta

Delta reflects the sensitivity of an option=s value to small changes in the price of the underlying asset. The delta of a call option is always a number between zero and one, and the delta of a put option is always a number between zero and minus one (some leveraged options may be exceptions to this rule). For example, consider a call option on a corporate bond. If the delta value for the call option were 0.5, the price of the option would be expected to increase by 50 cents if the price of the bond increased by $1. Likewise, a decrease of $1 in the price of the bond would be expected to cause a decrease of 50 cents in the price of the option.

Delta helps traders to hedge portfolios of financial instruments. The delta value indicates the amount of hedging required to neutralize the price risk arising from spot movements. Using the previous example, the $1 increase in the price of the corporate bond is equal to the price change for two call options (i.e., 2 times 50 cents). Consequently, if a trader=s portfolio were long one bond and hedged with two call options, it would not be affected by changes in the price of the bond. The ratio of the number of options of the same type (e.g., call options) to the number of underlying financial instruments is called the hedge ratio. In this example, the hedge ratio is 2:1, which is the inverse of the delta value for the option. A fully hedged portfolio, such as that described above, is called a delta-neutral portfolio. For such a portfolio, the change in the value of the options will be approximately offset by the change in the value of the underlying bond, as long as the change in the price of the underlying bond is small.

When the price of the underlying instrument changes by a small amount, the resulting change in the value of the option is reliably predicted by delta. When the value of the underlying instrument changes considerably, however, the delta itself will nearly always change. The size of the change in delta is predicted by gamma (described below). Thus, the manager of a delta-neutral portfolio must

constantly adjust the portfolio to reflect the changes in delta. This change in delta exposes options users to gamma risk.

Gamma

Gamma is a measure of the amount delta would change in response to a change in the price of the underlying instrument. Gamma thus provides a measure of the sensitivity of a delta-neutral portfolio. A gamma other than zero indicates that the delta would change when the price of the underlying instrument changes, implying that the number of options in the portfolio relative to the number of underlying instruments would need to be adjusted. As gamma increases, so does delta, and the more significant will be the portfolio adjustments required.

Gamma is the most important options measure for hedged options portfolios. Gamma tends to be lowest when a standard option is deep in the money or deep out of the money. Gamma tends to be highest when a standard option is at-the-money and near or at expiration; a small change in the spot price can make the difference between exercising an in-the-money option and letting a out-of-the-money option expire.

Because gamma is highest for at-the-money options, an options book is most apt to become unhedged if it contains near-the-money options, all else being equal. As the time to maturity decreases, the gamma of an at-the-money option approaches infinity. Therefore, at-the-money options are the most difficult options to hedge. Examiners should seek to understand how gamma is reported and managed by the financial institution, how it is used in the bank=s hedging strategies, and how it is used to evaluate the bank=s income from options trading (e.g., the frequency of the hedging interval and the use of dynamic hedging strategies).

Vega

Vega, also known as kappa, is a measure of the sensitivity of an option=s price to changes in the volatility of the price of the underlying instrument.

The value of an option largely depends on the likelihood that the price of the underlying instrument will keep or move the option in the money before the option matures. For example, the value of a call option is based on the likelihood that the price of the underlying instrument will surpass the strike price before the option expires. The more volatile the price of the underlying instrument, the greater the potential for its price movement. Because purchased options have asymmetric risk (i.e., potentially unlimited upside gain with limited downside cost), greater potential movement in the underlying instrument can benefit only options buyers. As a result, standard options, such as calls and puts, always increase in value with increases in the volatility of the underlying instrument.

Theta

Theta is a measure of the amount an option's price would be expected to change to reflect the passage of time (also called time decay). The value of an option depends on the likelihood that the price of the underlying instrument will change in the desired manner. The likelihood of a favorable event occurring decreases as time to expiration decreases. Consequently, the value of an option generally declines with the passage of time (which is advantageous to the writer but not to the holder of the option).

Rho

Rho is a measure of the amount an option's price would change for an incremental move (generally one basis point) in short-term interest rates. Rho is usually small compared with the other option price components, because interest rates rarely move enough to have an appreciable effect on option prices. The impact of rho is more significant for longer-term options or in-the-money options.

Risk Management of Financial Derivatives

Appendix C

Evaluating Models for Measuring Price Risk

Probability theory can be used to create models that describe the way market rates and prices move. These models can characterize the movement of a single price, as well as represent the relationship between one price and another. To assist examiners in the evaluation of probability models used in price risk measurement , general attributes of common models used by dealers are discussed below. Some banks employ a combination of models, using a common confidence interval, to measure risk for different derivative portfolios or products. For example, a dealer may use a variance/covariance matrix model to estimate its fixed income exposure. The bank may judge a simulation model to be better than the variance/covariance model at estimating its nonlinear exposures, such as options. Therefore, the results of a simulation could be used to estimate nonlinear risk such as might be found in an options portfolio, even though mixing models may make it difficult to aggregate measured risk exposure across portfolios.

No single approach is best or always appropriate. When determining whether a system is appropriate, banks should take into account the type of derivatives, the level of risk, and the board's expressed tolerance for risk.

Variance/Covariance Models

A variance/covariance model is one method of calculating a risk measure commonly referred to as value-at-risk (VAR). In the basic implementation of this model, the underlying probability theory assumes that knowledge of the variance of the portfolio=s value is sufficient to measure market risk of the portfolio. An estimate of the variance of the portfolio could be obtained from estimates of the variances of the values of every instrument in the portfolio as well as estimates of the co-movement or covariance of the values of every possible pair of instruments in the portfolio.

Because of the potentially enormous computational effort involved, a simplification is usually employed. In this simplification each instrument is associated with some market factors that determine the variance of the instrument=s value. For example, a bond=s price variance might be modeled as a specific sensitivity to each of six different forward interest rates, where a sensitivity describes how the bond price changes for, say, a 1-basis-point change in each market factor. Rather than estimate price variances for every instrument and all covariances between instruments, the calculation estimates the variances of market factors along with the covariances between the market factors. If many instruments are influenced by the same market factors (e.g., all bonds in the portfolio are affected by the same six rates), then the number of variances and covariances to be estimated will be much reduced.

The set of market factors used differs among institutions. Methods of specifying sensitivities to market factors also differ across institutions, especially where it is not possible to price exactly an instrument in terms of a set of given sensitivities to market factors. Many methods are used to estimate the variances and covariances of market factors, and different methods will give different estimates. Which method is best for which factors is a question of ongoing debate.

Using estimates of the variances of these market factors, the sensitivities of portfolio instruments to each factor, and the size of the position in each instrument, the portfolio variance is computed. The formula for computing a portfolio variance in this way is derived from statistics theory and is usually written in matrix notation, which is why the variance/covariance model is sometimes referred to as the variance/covariance matrix model (or less accurately as the correlation matrix model).

The final step in deriving the estimated market risk of the portfolio is to multiply the estimated portfolio standard deviation (square root of the variance) by a number, such as 2, e.g., a two-standard-deviation move. This multiplication factor is based on probability theory of the normal distribution, and serves to identify the magnitude of the change in portfolio value that is to be called the VAR. For any normal distribution the probability of an outcome can be stated as some multiple of the standard deviation. For example, approximately 97.5 percent of all changes will be less in magnitude than a change in value equal to two standard deviations. This relationship does not hold if the portfolio distribution is not normal. The multiplier used differs by institution.

Some institutions also multiply the portfolio standard deviation by a factor to reflect the risk of portfolio holding periods longer than one day. The multiplier varies by institution, but is always the square root of the length of the holding period. The square-root rule is derived from probability theory and is a valid way of scaling up the one-day portfolio standard deviation under some circumstances.

In the basic implementation of the variance/covariance method, it is not possible to take into account nonlinear (e.g., option) exposures when measuring price risk. However, various extensions of the basic implementation are used by banks to attempt to capture those exposures.

The approaches vary and are influenced by the nature and extent of nonlinear exposures in the portfolio.

Historical Simulation Models

The historical simulation model is another approach to measuring VAR. This model does not assume that the portfolio variance (or any other parameter(s)) is sufficient for measuring risk. For this reason, these models are called nonparametric. In this model each instrument in the portfolio is repriced a specified number of times, each time using a set of pricing inputs collected from a different day in the past. For example, if 250 different portfolio values are desired, then 250 days of pricing inputs are required. For pricing a vanilla European option (holder can only exercise the option on expiration day), then, the price of the underlying, the appropriate tenor volatility of the underlying, and the yield curve are collected on 250 different days. Each of the 250 portfolio values is obtained simply by adding up the values of the individual instruments obtained using one day=s data. By using one day=s data to reprice the entire portfolio each time, the actual correlations between the instruments in the portfolio are embedded in the risk measure. Because this method reprices each instrument for each set of inputs, nonlinear (e.g., options) exposures are more readily incorporated into the measure of price risk than under the basic variance/covariance method.

It is assumed that the relative values and frequencies of these sets of pricing inputs collected from history are representative of the distribution of possible values of these sets of inputs over the next day (assuming a one-day holding period). This assumption is implicit in the basic variance/covariance model as well. For each set of pricing inputs, the instruments in the portfolio are repriced and the portfolio value is recalculated. These hypothetical portfolio values are then ranked from lowest to highest and the value corresponding to the desired percentile of the distribution of portfolio values is selected as the estimate of the price risk or VAR. (The reported price risk is sometimes stated as the difference between the current value of the portfolio and this particular hypothetical value.)

Because the computational cost of repricing each instrument in the portfolio many times can be great, fast pricing approximations are sometimes used for some instruments. Although better estimates of market risk are sometimes obtained by using a greater number of days of historical data, computation costs rise as well. The number of days of historical pricing inputs used by banks varies greatly. The number of days of inputs necessary to obtain a reasonable estimate of the price risk will depend on the bank=s experience with its own portfolio.

Monte Carlo Methods

Monte Carlo is another form of simulation. It may be considered to be a hybrid form of the variance/covariance and historical simulation methods, because it is usually a simulation based on a parametric probability model that uses a variance/covariance matrix of market factors. This method therefore has the potential to share the advantages and drawbacks of each of the other two methods. Monte Carlo implementations can vary enormously. The general approach is as follows: First, assume a parametric probability model for the future value of the portfolio using the same market factor idea used in the variance/covariance method. Second, obtain estimates of the necessary parameters (e.g., variances and covariances) from historical data. Third, generate some number of hypothetical sets of future values of the market factors by employing a random number generator that uses the estimated variances and covariances. Fourth, revalue the portfolio for each set of hypothetical future values of the market factors. Fifth, choose that portfolio value corresponding to the desired percentile of the resulting hypothetical distribution of future portfolio values.

While increasing the number of simulations increases the precision of the estimate of risk, the cost in additional calculation time can be relatively high. For example, statistical theory shows that doubling the accuracy of the estimated VAR in a Monte Carlo requires that the number of sets of hypothetical future portfolio values be quadrupled.

Risk Management
of Financial Derivatives
Appendix D

Evaluating Price Risk Measurement

Most banks use a combination of independent validation, calibration, back-testing, and reserves to manage potential weaknesses in price risk measurement models. These processes are described below.

Validation

Validation is the process through which 1) the internal logic of the model is evaluated (includes verification of mathematical accuracy), 2) model predictions are compared with subsequent events, and 3) the model is compared with other existing models, internal and external (when available). New models both internally developed and purchased from vendors should receive initial validation reviews. Internally developed models may require more intensive evaluation because they may not have been market-tested by external parties. Thereafter, the frequency and extent to which models are validated depends on changes that affect pricing or risk presentation and on the existing control environment. Changes in market conditions that affect pricing and risk conventions, and therefore model performance, should trigger additional validation review.

Risk management policies should clearly address the scope of the validation process, frequency of validations, documentation requirements, and management responses. At a minimum, policies should require the evaluation of significant underlying algorithms and assumptions before the model is put in regular use, and as market conditions warrant thereafter. Such internal evaluations should be conducted by parties who are independent of the business using or developing the model, where practicable. The evaluation may, if necessary, be conducted or supplemented with reviews by qualified outside parties, such as experts in highly technical models and risk management techniques.

Calibration

One calibrates a model in two steps. First, one ensures that the model is internally consistent B that is, that the internal logic is sound. Second, one observes market prices to adjust the model parameters. For example, if the model prices are below market prices for caps and floors, it is likely that the model=s assumed volatility is below that of the market. Repeatedly adjusting the volatility of other model parameters until model prices match market prices is called convergence to market.

Back-Testing

Back-testing is a method of periodically evaluating the accuracy and predictive capability of a bank=s risk measurement system. There is no widely agreed-upon process for back-testing and techniques are continuing to evolve. Back-testing usually involves an ex *post* comparison of a bank=s profits and losses for a particular day against the risk measure projected by the model for the same day.

When evaluating back-testing results, it is important to understand the complexities of comparing risk measures and daily P&L. For banks using VAR models, one significant issue to consider is that VAR assumes a static trading portfolio that is not adjusted during the trading day, while actual P&L incorporates results of intraday trading. Thus, comparisons of VAR to actual P&L need to address the effect of intraday trading and risk management activities, customer mark-up, and net interest income. Because of the limitations of using actual P&L, some banks have elected to use hypothetical P&L that excludes customer mark-up, intraday trading profits and losses, and net interest income.

There are other issues to consider when reconciling risk measurement results with daily P&L. Exceptions may occur because of sudden changes in volatilities or correlations caused by large shifts in the market. Operational issues such as incorrect data entry, subsequent P&L adjustments, and timing differences can also give rise to differences between risk measures and daily P&L results.

Risk management policies should address the scope of the back-testing process, frequency of back-testing, documentation requirements, and management responses. To be most effective, back-testing should be conducted regularly by parties independent of those developing or using the model. Results of back-testing should be part of risk management reporting to senior management.

Reserves for Model Risk

Banks should consider establishing reserves for model risk. These reserves may be appropriate for models measuring the price risk of complex instruments or models using unconventional valuation techniques that are not widely accepted in the market. These reserves are normally established through adjustments to mid-market valuations. If the bank elects to establish reserves for model risk, policies should require documentation of rationale, require periodic review of assumptions, and provide for proper accounting treatment. See the ATransaction Risk@ section for more information.

Risk Management
of Financial Derivatives
Appendix E

Stress Testing

Tier I and Tier II dealers with large positions relative to earnings and capital should regularly supplement their daily risk management information with stress testing or simulations that show how the portfolio might perform during certain extreme events or highly volatile markets. To perform stress testing, a dealer=s risk measurement system must be flexible enough to facilitate running various scenarios. Assumptions used in the stress scenario should be carefully constructed to test the portfolio=s vulnerabilities. It is common for banks to model stress tests around large historical market moves. However, large market moves do not always produce the greatest losses or expose a portfolio=s vulnerabilities. For example, for some option portfolios, the worst scenario could result from a very small change in the price of the underlying assets.

The more sophisticated risk management systems will identify potential scenarios that would produce the most undesirable results and estimate the probability of their occurrence. Depending on the severity of the outcomes and the likelihood of occurrence, management should take appropriate initiatives to reduce risk. Stress testing should involve both the risk control unit and the trading desk, as their perspectives will be complimentary. Traders= input is valuable to the process as they are generally the most knowledgeable about the portfolio=s vulnerabilities. The participation of risk control provides independent oversight and an objective viewpoint to assure the integrity of the process.

The framework for stress testing should be detailed in the risk management policy. Results of stress testing scenarios along with major assumptions should be provided to the board and senior management on a periodic basis. This information should include an assessment of the bank=s ability to effectively respond to the event and assumptions underlying this assessment.

Risk Management of Financial Derivatives

Appendix F

Interconnection Risk

Dealers with high price risk should supplement stress testing with an analysis of their exposure to interconnection risk. While stress testing typically considers the movement of a single market factor (e.g., interest rates), interconnection risk considers the linkages *across* markets (e.g., interest rates and foreign exchange rates) and across the various categories of risk (e.g., price, credit, and liquidity risk). For example, stress from one market may transmit shocks to other markets and give rise to otherwise dormant risks. Evaluating interconnected risk involves assessing the total or aggregate impact of singular events.

Management must understand how risks are connected in order to avoid disasters like those encountered in the 1980s. During that decade, many Texas banks failed to see the correlation between real estate prices and the profitability of the oil industry. Similarly, banks lending to less-developed countries (LDC) failed to see the link between world commodity prices and the LDC debt repayment capacity.

To understand interconnection risk, banks should regularly evaluate alternative market situations using scenario or what-if analyses. For example, a scenario analysis might assess the results of various twists and shifts of the yield curve, as well as changes in the relationships among yield curves for various interest rates. Questions that should be addressed include:

- What happens to the value of financial instruments?

- Given what you know about counterparty activities, how might the counterparty=s credit quality be affected?

- What might happen to market liquidity if the change indicated by the scenario occurred suddenly rather than more gradually?

- What possible condition of the macro economy might also accompany the shift and/or twist used in a particular scenario (e.g., an inverted yield curve sometimes signals an oncoming economic downturn)?

Issues for review might include:

- The volatility of prospective earnings and capital.

- The extent to which net funding requirements become concentrated around certain dates.

- Potential extensions of holding and settlement periods.

- Impact of credit reserves, and potential changes for administrative and close-out costs.

Sophisticated banks should be developing and evaluating methods to identify, measure, monitor, and control exposures from activities that are interconnected. Senior management and the board should consider interconnection risk when evaluating the bank's overall risk profile, setting limits, and overseeing day-to-day activity.

Risk Management of Financial Derivatives

Appendix G

Fundamental Issues B Price Risk Measurement Systems

There are six fundamental issues that must be addressed when formulating price risk measurement systems. These are: (1) purpose of the measure; (2) position description; (3) holding period; (4) confidence interval (probability threshold); (5) historical time period of the data series; (6) aggregation.

Purpose of the Measure

For most dealers, the price risk measurement system is designed to provide a sense of the overnight exposure to potential adverse changes in the major factors affecting the value of the institution's positions. Thus, the systems generally reflect exposure in what is considered a normal market environment. However, banks may modify the price risk measurement models for capital allocation purposes. For example, a bank may use a longer holding period for capital allocation purposes than to manage daily risk because capital is generally intended to be a cushion against unexpected losses. Therefore, banks may use more conservative assumptions, reflecting extreme market movements, when estimating price risk for their capital allocation models.

Banks with significant price risk exposure may be subject to the risk-based capital requirements for market (price) risk under 12 CFR 3, appendix B. This rule allows banks to use their own internal VAR models to measure market (price) risk exposure subject to parameters discussed in the appendix (e.g., specified holding periods, confidence levels, historical period of data series). As mentioned above, it is unlikely that the subject banks would use these same parameters for day-to-day risk management purposes because of the differing uses and purpose of the price risk measurement information. See the ACapital Issues@ section for more information on the market risk rule.

Position Description

A critical step in developing a price risk measurement system is establishing the framework by which positions will be described. There must be agreement on a standard method of describing risk across businesses. For example, a forward foreign exchange component can be described in two ways:

- As a specific *product*; or

- As a combination of price risk *factors* C in this case, spot foreign exchange rates and interest rates.

The more sophisticated systems attempt to break instruments into their component parts using price risk factors. These systems attempt to estimate the bank's exposure to the principal factors affecting the value of their positions. This approach has important advantages. First, it enables the institution to aggregate its exposure to a specific factor, such as interest rates, across all products. Second, it can generally capture new products or structures more easily. This is a clear advantage for banks that engage in structured OTC derivatives for which specific prices are not readily available.

The risk measurement process frequently requires that a firm's positions be mapped onto a grid. This mapping is done both by tenor and by long (asset) position or short (liability) position class. Care must be taken to ensure that exposures are sufficiently similar to merit their inclusion in the same class. The greater the mapping detail, the greater the accuracy of the measure. However, greater detail increases the time it takes to perform the necessary calculations. Once the descriptive mechanism is in place, risk measurement systems extract the information they need from the systems used by traders to price and manage their positions. (Note: This mapping process may also be done by the trading system.)

Holding Period

Typically, banks measure the risk of loss using the change in market value over a one-day holding period. For many traded instruments, the position exposure can be eliminated in a matter of hours (perhaps minutes). However, for some less-liquid instruments, several days or weeks may be needed for an orderly reduction in position exposure.

Most models are relatively sensitive to the holding period assumption. In order to convert the system to a cost to close or other measure, a number of assumptions must be made regarding market behavior, acceptable offsets and their likelihood of being executed, and trader capabilities. These assumptions are relatively less empirical than those derived from historical observation or simulation. The one-day holding period provides a starting point for discussion. When establishing limits, banks using a one-day holding period will need to incorporate judgments about liquidity and other events and make any adjustments deemed necessary.

An important exception should be made for sectors in which there are significant concerns regarding event or liquidity risk, or in which historical data are unreliable. This exception occurs most notably in emerging markets debt. Here, considerations regarding the magnitude of event risk, as well as uncertainty regarding market depth, tend to argue for longer holding periods. Additionally, activities involving relatively illiquid instruments, or instruments for which good data may not be available, may need additional limits tailored to the specific attributes of that business.

Ultimately, the length of a holding period depends on the purpose of the system and its place in the overall risk management process. Most banks clearly state that the measurement system is designed to be an indicator of what can be expected under normal conditions. It is only one of several tools used to monitor exposure on an ongoing basis. It becomes the starting point for further discussion.

Confidence Interval

The confidence interval, also referred to as the probability threshold, specifies how frequently the estimate provided by the model will likely be surpassed. Specifying a confidence interval of 99 percent is more conservative than an interval of 95 percent. With the 99 percent interval, actual results will likely surpass the model's measured amount roughly once every 100 days. With the 95 percent threshold, the results will surpass the model's estimate roughly five times every 100 days (or once every 20 days, at least once a month). Confidence intervals are frequently expressed in terms of standard deviations. (E.g., actual results will likely exceed the model=s estimate if rates move in excess of two standard deviations, which is approximately a 95 percent interval.) The confidence interval is critical to interpreting both the level of exposure and size of risk limits. Ultimately, the choice of a confidence interval should be consistent with the purpose of the measure and the limit structure. For example, banks choosing to lower the confidence interval would also be expected to lower their risk limits, assuming their risk tolerance had not changed.

Data Series

When using risk measurement models, banks must select the data series that will be the basis for market volatility and correlation assumptions. Among the many issues to consider when selecting the data series are the source, time horizon, frequency of updating, and time-of-day.

The data series can be obtained by using historical data or data implied by current market rates. Although each source has its advantages depending on market conditions, historical data are most commonly used.

The length of the time horizon over which to collect the data should depend upon the relevance of past periods to the current market conditions and to what extent recent market events will be incorporated. During volatile markets, using a longer time horizon may understate risk because the risk measure will be slower to adjust. A shorter time horizon will make the risk measure adjust more quickly to changing market conditions. Another issue to consider when selecting a data series is whether to exclude certain data points, such as those depicting extreme low-probability events. Inclusion of outliers may overstate risk during stable market conditions. On the other hand, failure to include past data that reflects unusual or higher than normal price volatility may lead to understated risk estimates.

The frequency with which data are sampled must also be determined. The frequency should be high enough to produce a statistically valid sample. The time of day that data are collected should also be considered (e.g., end of day, intraday, high/low).

In selecting the parameters for the data series it is important to understand that there is no single right answer. The meaningfulness of results will vary with market conditions.

Aggregation

A number of issues should be addressed when aggregating exposures to produce a consolidated measure. One of the most important issues is determining the extent to which exposures within markets (e.g., currency markets) and across markets (e.g., currency and interest rate markets) move together or are correlated. The correlation coefficient, which changes in relation to the strength of the relationship between movements in two price risk variables, represents the likelihood of the two variables moving together. The coefficient ranges from -1 to 1. The stronger the relationship between the two variables, the closer the coefficient is to 1 or -1. Correlation coefficients can be based on historical data or implied from current market conditions.

The extent to which banks use correlations in risk measurement systems varies widely. Therefore, the risk measurement results for similar portfolios can be very different depending on correlation assumptions. Most commonly, correlations are used within markets. It is less common, because of systems limitations, for correlations to be used across markets. One complication of correlating exposures is that correlations may be unstable in volatile markets. Generally, the use of lower correlations will reflect reduced portfolio risk. However, by using lower correlations, the model may underestimate risk during volatile markets. If a bank chooses to use correlations when aggregating risks, the analysis should be empirically derived and updated regularly.

When consolidating institutional exposure, the assumption will frequently be made that exposures are not correlated. When assumptions are made that exposures are not correlated, they are generally aggregated using the square root of the sum of the squares method, which is a widely used statistical approach to aggregating portfolio value.

Banks may also aggregate exposure using a combination of risk measurement methods based on a characteristic of the underlying instrument. For example, the interest rate risk from fixed income positions based on a variance/covariance model may be aggregated with the interest rate risk from option positions based on a simulation model. The feature that makes the measures comparable is the defined confidence interval.

In developing a consolidated risk measure, banks will make a number of trade-offs. Trade-offs are most significant at institutions that have decentralized trading environments, are active in several countries and time zones, or operate (often because of mergers) using a variety of computer systems. Given a clear definition of the system's purpose, however, the problems are not insurmountable. The main consideration is time. Because of the complexity of some products and the number of calculations required, compromises and approximations are required in order to obtain a timely estimate of aggregate risk. Institutions must continually evaluate assumptions and simplified position descriptions. Data requirements should be incorporated in longer-term technology plans.

Risk Management of Financial Derivatives

Appendix H

Credit Risk Add-On

Typically, a dealer or active position-taker=s determination of the credit risk add-on will take one of two approaches: (1) transaction level or (2) portfolio level. These approaches are described below.

Transaction-Level Approach

The transaction-level approach computes either peak or average potential credit exposure. Peak exposure is measured as the largest historical price movement or a statistically remote outcome such as a two- or three-standard-deviation price move. It can be derived from a series of possible outcomes, each with a probability of occurrence. The mean of these probability-weighted outcomes is the average exposure. Peak exposure reflects a more conservative assessment of potential credit risk; bank management should be prepared to justify the use of average exposure in calculating the credit risk add-on. The transaction-level approach treats derivatives individually and presumes the total exposure in the portfolio to be the sum of the potential exposures for each transaction.

Under the transaction-level approach, the credit risk for any given counterparty is determined by adding, for each transaction, the replacement cost (zero, if the mark-to-market is negative) to the calculated credit add-on. If the bank has legally enforceable close-out netting arrangements, it may net mark-to-market exposures for each counterparty (taking advantage of contracts with negative mark-to-market values), but add-ons should not be netted against negative mark-to-markets unless the bank is using simulation modeling to assess the entire credit exposure to a given counterparty. Summing the replacement cost and add-on will result in the loan equivalent calculation of credit risk for each derivative contract. Bank management should establish guidelines and maintain documentation to support the assumptions used in these credit calculations and simulation analyses. The assumptions and variables used must be kept current. Moreover, major systems should be validated at least once a year, consistent with the validation process for price risk measurement systems described in appendix D.

Portfolio Approach

Because the transaction-level approach ignores portfolio offsets or the probability that all transactions will not be at the peak or average exposure at the same time, it overstates the risk in the aggregate portfolio. Therefore, some banks use the portfolio approach to measure potential credit exposure. The portfolio approach uses simulation modeling to calculate exposures through time for each counterparty. For example, the master agreement may specify that a default on any one transaction is considered a default on all transactions by the counterparty. Accordingly, when netting is allowed, the expected exposure (close-out) amount is the net of all positive and negative replacement costs with each counterparty.

Risk Management of Financial Derivatives

Appendix I

Netting Arrangements

Netting is an agreement between counterparties to offset positions or obligations. The three primary forms of netting are settlement netting, default netting, and multilateral netting. Each of these netting methods is discussed below.

Close-Out Netting

Close-out (or default) netting is a bilateral agreement intended to reduce presettlement credit risk in the event that a counterparty becomes insolvent before the settlement date. Upon default, the nondefaulting party nets gains and losses with the defaulting counterparty to a single payment for all covered transactions.

Settlement Netting

Settlement (or payment) netting is a bilateral agreement intended to reduce settlement risk. Settlement netting is a mechanism in which parties agree to net payments payable between them on any date in the same currency under the same transaction or a specified group of transactions. Unlike close-out netting, payment netting is continual during the life of a master agreement.

Multilateral Netting

Multilateral netting is designed to extend the benefits of bilateral netting to cover contracts with a group of counterparties. Commonly, under a multilateral netting arrangement, a clearinghouse interposes itself as the legal counterparty for covered contracts transacted between its members. Multilateral netting is used in the clearing and settlement of contracts on futures exchanges.

Risk Management of Financial Derivatives

Appendix J

Credit Enhancements

The use of credit enhancements such as collateral, margin, and third-party guarantees with OTC derivatives is becoming more common. The growth of credit enhancement arrangements has been driven, in part, by the desire of lower-rated or unrated counterparties to access the derivatives market.

Although credit enhancements can be used to manage counterparty credit risk, these mechanisms should be considered a secondary source of repayment in lieu of the counterparty's ability to meet cash flow demands through its ongoing operations. The existence of credit enhancements does not transform a poor credit risk into a good one.

Although the concepts of collateral and margin are similar, there are some important differences. A margining agreement requires that cash or very liquid securities be deposited immediately with the counterparty. After the initial deposit, margin accounts are revalued and settled daily. If the margin account falls below a predetermined level (the maintenance margin), the other counterparty receives a margin call and is required to post additional margin. In the event of default, the counterparty holding the margin can liquidate the margin account.

Collateral arrangements typically require perfecting a lien and hypothecating securities or other assets. The range of assets eligible under collateral arrangements is usually wider than that under margining arrangements. Often the posting of collateral is subject to credit exposure thresholds. In this instance, the counterparty would only have to post collateral after the credit exposure reached a certain agreed-upon level. Revaluation of collateral may be less frequent than that required under margining agreements (however, revaluation of collateral should be commensurate with the volatility of the exposure, nature of collateral pledged and degree of excess coverage). Settlement of collateral shortfalls may also be less frequent than under margining arrangements.

There are many issues to consider when entering into collateral or margin agreements. Transaction, compliance, and liquidity issues can become complex depending on the type, volume, and location of collateral or margin.

The bank's credit policies and procedures, depending on whether the bank is a provider or receiver of collateral or margin, should address:

- Acceptable types of instruments for collateral and margin.

- Collateral or margin concentration limits by issuer, country, industry, or asset class.

- Correlation of the price sensitivity of the collateral or margin with the underlying transaction.

- Substitution of assets.

- Timing of posting (at inception, upon change in risk rating, upon change in the level of exposure, etc.).

- Valuation methods (e.g., sources of prices, frequency of revaluation, haircuts).

- Permissibility to hypothecate or rehypothecate collateral.

- Physical control over collateral.

- Dispute resolution.

Operating procedures should ensure proper control over the assigned assets and the timely assessment of the value relative to the amount of credit exposure. There is a tendency for the market to require collateral and margin arrangements from lesser-rated banks. However, in order to avoid potential credit perception problems, two-way or bilateral arrangements among banks are encouraged. These arrangements would require both parties to provide collateral based on the value of their contracts at a specified point in time. A bank should evaluate the counterparty's ability to provide and meet collateral or margin requirements at inception and during the term of the agreement.

The use of credit enhancement agreements to build up a bank=s price-risk-taking or interest-rate-risk-taking position may present safety and soundness concerns. A bank should engage in such activities only after affirming that its liquidity position will not be compromised, especially under stress scenarios, and that a satisfactory balance exists within its overall risk profile.

Risk Management
of Financial Derivatives
Appendix K

Early Termination Agreements

To reduce potential exposure, banks may enter into contracts that include early termination agreements. If a triggering event occurs (e.g., credit rating downgrade of a counterparty), the master agreement is terminated. Thus, before an actual default can occur, an early termination agreement allows the bank to reduce or eliminate its exposure to a particular counterparty. Although obtaining an early termination agreement from a counterparty can reduce credit exposure, providing an early termination trigger to a counterparty can increase liquidity and price risk. Banks should carefully control the volume and circumstances of transactions in which they may become subject to early termination agreements.

Risk Management
of Financial Derivatives

References

Laws

Employee Retirement Income Security Act
Federal Deposit Insurance Corporation Improvement Act of
1991,
     Sections 401 through 407
Financial Institutions Reform, Recovery, and Enforcement Act of
1989
U.S. Bankruptcy Code

Regulations

12 CFR 3, Appendixes A and B

OCC Issuances

Banking Circular 277, ᴀRisk Management of Financial
Derivatives@
Comptroller=s Handbook, ᴀFutures Commission Merchant
Activities@
Comptroller=s Handbook, ᴀEmerging Market Country Products
and
     Trading Activities@
Comptroller=s Handbook, ᴀInterest Rate Risk@
OCC Bulletin 94-32, ᴀQuestions and Answers About BC-277@
OCC Advisory Letter 94-2, ᴀPurchases of Structured Notes@
OCC Bulletin 96-25, ᴀFiduciary Risk Management of Derivatives
and
     Mortgage-Backed Securities@
OCC Bulletin 96-36, ᴀInterest Rate Risk@
OCC Bulletin 96-43, ᴀCredit Derivatives@

www.ingramcontent.com/pod-product-compliance
Lightning Source LLC
Chambersburg PA
CBHW080248290526
45790CB00005B/1739